BEST OF
THE BREWER

FAVORITES FROM THE FIRST DECADE OF
FRESH FROM THE BREWER COLUMNS

TROY A. BREWER

aventine press

Published by Aventine Press
55 East Emerson St.
Chula Vista CA 91911
www.aventinepress.com

ISBN: 978-1-59330-869-8

Library of Congress Control Number: 2014918046
Library of Congress Cataloging-in-Publication Data
Best of The Brewer/ Troy A Brewer

Printed in the United States of America

To Leanna

I dedicate this book of my best columns to the lady who has always seen the best in me while living with the worst of me.

Leanna, you really are the very best of all the Brewers.
Troy

TABLE OF CONTENTS

The Brewer with one of his kids at the SPARKWORLDWIDE. ORG orphanage in Uganda, East Africa.

INTRODUCTION

There are some really great writers in this world; unfortunately, I am not one of them.

I can spin a yarn though, and I do have fairly competent people who when sober, can decipher and translate my hieroglyphics into legible reading.

After all the dust settles and the machines stop turning, most of it is actually worth reading and some of it is worth reading several times over. God is still in the miracle working business.

I like to write. Actually, I love to write. I carry around journals with me, partly because I love to learn and mostly because I love to write. Sometimes passion moves something into greatness before talent does. It's my passion for the Pen that makes my stuff worth reading, I think. I am addicted to Ink like an over compulsive tattoo artist.

God tends to use compulsiveness and hone them into skills of passion. Because of this, the truth is that you don't have to be great to really be great.

Is Willie Nelson a great singer? No, and if you don't believe me listen to what a train wreck he sounds like next to Julio Iglesias in "to all the girls I've loved before." But to millions of people, it doesn't matter if he is a great singer or not, He's just great.

He's Willie Nelson and the part of the world I come from, which is the part of the world he comes from, thinks he's just great.

THE MAD HEIFER

When I was 17, a friend and I cut the top off of a ancient 1954 Pontiac star chief. We pulled it out of a back pasture with a tractor, painted it like a cow and put horns on the front grill. After nearly a month and $800, we got the engine to crank and the transmission to turn. All that hard work and hooplah just so we could drive something crazy to Willie's picnic. The somewhat-annual Willie Nelson Fourth of July Picnic, a tradition unique to Texas, was something like a redneck Woodstock and right up my alley in the early 1980s.

Going to Austin was like going to the moon for me back then and we flew into town like the spaceship Columbia. We somehow made it to Southpark Meadows, an outdoor venue on the west side of I-35, with only one gear left and something black coming out of our tailpipe.

Willie closed the night and at least a thousand of us opted to spend the night in the parking lot. It took me a whole other day to get back home because, The mad heifer, my car, died sometime in the night and I left its carcass in the south meadows parking lot, never to be seen again.

I tell that story now to say that not a single one of us thought Willie's nasal serenade was beautiful, but we all thought the show was great. We all thought Willie was great.

Just like that, you could put my writing up beside Truman Capote, Harper Lee or Larry McMurty and I might look like a train wreck too. But like Willie, I do not care to try and be any of those people. On most days it feels good to be me. It is all I have to work with, so I might as well be happy with it.

TRUE TO FORM

I write my newspaper columns like I am, and as a person I might seem a bit complicated even contradicting. No, really I am straight forward simple just richly diverse. I would argue against me being complicated.

All of my columns are pro Jesus and have a Christian punch line because that's the way I am. Since my first life changing encounter with Jesus Christ, I remain a non-apologetic drop-dead-sold-out-Jesus Freak. I am the Christian the devil warned you about. I am unafraid to admit I want to use whatever influence I have to direct people into looking up Jesus for themselves.

What seems to trip up a lot of people is that my columns are not churchy. What I mean is that they tend to be secular sounding. This is on purpose because I don't see a line between the sacred and secular. All of life belongs to God and God can be seen in all of life, if you have an eye to look.

I choose to do just that and a newspaper is the perfect place to spout off modern pop culture, strange ideas and ancient lore while pointing out Jesus in all of that. Fresh from the Brewer is column that attempts this.

UNDERSTANDING THE AUDIENCE

Ministry is only effective when you are willing to serve the people you are ministering to. Jesus said «If anyone wants to be first, he must be the very last, and the servant of all.»

Authority and making a difference in somebody's life does not come from being the meanest or the smartest or the loudest but in the Kingdom, it actually comes from a willingness to serve.

A lot of really good Pastors don't understand why the newspaper won't print their brilliant bible study and it is because they don't understand the audience.

You have to actually care as much about your readers as you care about Jesus. This, in the bible, is referred to as the great commandment.

Billy Graham pulled it off in a way that is better than anybody I have seen. He learned to focus his anointing and target an audience for a specific outcome. -Salvation.

He has been greatly criticized by untold religious folk for not preaching a deeper word. While the self-appointed "watchmen on the walls" were busy critiquing him, the Billy Graham Evangelistic Association reports, «nearly 215 million people in more than 185 countries» have been reached through his ministry. In his lifetime, he has led untold thousands and thousands to make a decision to receive Jesus as personal Savior and to live for Christ.

Now the Brewer is no Billy Graham. BUT the majority of hate mail I have received through the years over the columns you are about to read, have not been from atheists, witches or recovering zombies. -But rather the chosen frozen.

People think that because I love people who are obviously messed up, that I approve and endorse how they are messed up. Jesus was accused of the same thing.

The major criticism has mostly been that there is only one bible verse in a column of nearly 900 words. Yes, that is true. If you want to read something with lots of scripture, I say "Get a bible". There are 31,102, I think is the latest most accurate count, in a King James and I highly recommend it.

I have written a lot of theological books and this is not one of them. My newspaper columns are totally devoted and all about the really cool story I am trying to write about. It is also intended to be a Trojan horse with key elements of the heart of the King. After all, my name is Troy.

I want to point out how awesome the heart of Jesus is, not the bible, in my columns. If you want to read some of my bible thumping stuff, **Numbers that Preach** is a good place to start.

It took me over 20 years of studying the bible to put that book together and it doesn't make me mad that my not quite Christian friends won't read it. It doesn't interest them.

DANG INTERESTING

Some words that go along with interest are words like arouse, elicit, enkindle, evoke, fire, raise, & provoke. So why not write something interesting for the audience you intend on reading it?

Well, I'm trying anyway and so I write about things that interest me. Hopefully the enthusiasm will translate. It's not arrogance it is a type of *gonzo style* writing that is meant to be funny when need be and serious when need be.

I think there are a lot of really cool stories worth telling and far too many told that need to be swept back under the rock it crawled out from under.

200 CHANNELS

Music, science, history, people, war, the word, eating, relationships, disasters, sex. Nothing is off limits and yes I want to see the Kingdom in all of it.

So hate if you must, and be tormented with jealousy and envy as I have more fun than the law of Moses allows. I understand. Join a long line of miserable loathers or kick back with a stadium of fans and actually enjoy this small collection of the first Ten years of *Fresh from the Brewer.*

Who knows. You might even tell some of these stories with other people. Even worse, you might start seeing Jesus in everything around you too. That makes you really dangerous - and useful in the Kingdom.

Thanks for putting up with me and keep looking up.

Troy

The Brewer likes to dabble with Bees.

CHAPTER ONE
AMAZING PEOPLE

Sometimes, if you catch me on a well caffeinated day, I really like people.

I remember several years back, coming out of a movie house after watching a supernatural thriller about a boy who sees dead people everywhere. As I put my key in the car door, I said, "Thank you Jesus that from the time I was a little boy, I have seen live people."

It doesn't take an extra gift or a 6th sense to see dead people, but it takes the Holy Spirit Himself to give you an eye for life. Call me crazy, but I see live people. They are everywhere.

I have always had heroes and have studied people's exploits. In living a radical life for Jesus you tend to notice world changers and people who really make a difference.

People who really make a difference are people well acquainted with risk and I love people who are willing to take risks for what everybody else says cannot be achieved.

Helen Keller, world famous overcomer of what otherwise would have been a sightless, soundless and worse, wordless existence, said this;

"Security is mostly a superstition. It does not exist in nature, nor do the children of men as a whole experience it. Avoiding danger is no safer in the long run than outright exposure. Life is either a daring adventure, or nothing."

What follows is a collection of columns on people who have caught my eye through the years. These articles have been printed at different times, some of them, many years apart but these are on people whose lives have really gotten my attention.

This happens in the Kingdom. In fact, making a big deal out of people comes from the Kingdom.

...And what more shall I say? For the time would fail me to tell of Gideon and Barak and Samson and Jephthah, also of David and Samuel and the prophets: 33 who through faith subdued kingdoms, worked righteousness, obtained promises, stopped the mouths of lions, 34 quenched the violence of fire, escaped the edge of the sword, out of weakness were made strong, became valiant in battle, turned to fight the armies of the alien....
HEBREWS 11:32-34

So learn to have heroes and make a big deal if there be any virtue, if there is a good report. Enjoy the extraordinary stories about very common people.

"Tell the story that's been growing in your heart, the characters you can't keep out of your head, the tale story that speaks to you, that pops into your head during your daily commute, that wakes you up in the morning." – Jennifer Weiner

THE RIGHT PLACE AT THE RIGHT TIME

PARKED IN THE RIGHT SPOT

December first 1955 could have been a typical day but because the right person with the right character was in the right place at the right time, it was a day that changed the nation.

When Rosa Parks refused to give up her seat to a white man that demanded it, she was physically tired from a long day of work but she was spiritually and emotionally full of enough strength to push America out of the stone age of racism.

The rest of Rosa's story is history...her arrest and trial, a 381-day Montgomery Alabama bus boycott and the Supreme Court's ruling in November 1956 that segregation on transportation is unconstitutional.

Sometimes heroes come in small packages and her fight was not just for her race but also for everyone that is in love with what is right and hates what's wrong.

I thank God that Rosa didn't miss that bus. As sorry as I am for what she went through, I am so grateful that it was she on that bus in 1955. Everything changed because the right person was at the right place at the right time.

WILLING AND ABLE BECAUSE SHE WAS STABLE

She was able to do what God had destined her to do because she was willing to be who God had called her to be. Her character and strength put her into that world changing bus seat.

Parks' belief in God and her religious convictions are at the core of everything she did. It was the overriding theme of her book and the message she wanted to impart.

"I'd like for people to know that I had a very spiritual background and that I believe in church and my faith and that has helped to give me the strength and courage to live as I did."

The Brewer salutes you Rosa, and thanks God for you.

People of all races are amazing; they want the front of the bus, the middle of the road, and the back of the church. They want to push others out of the way to jockey themselves into positions of greatness but truth be told, your obedience to God will put you in amazing places that you couldn't have set up on your own with a million dollars.

TEA AND CRUMPETS

On my 2nd mission trip to Uganda east Africa, my wife and I had a typical 16-hour layover in London England. We took a train into downtown and ran around gawking at all things British.

Standing on the side of a busy London street and trying to make myself look right instead of left, I saw a police escort coming down the road towards me. There was a pretty good traffic jam that caused the entourage to stop right where Leanna and I were standing. Distracted by the obnoxious English siren, I finally looked into the back seat of the limousine closest to me. And there, not five feet away sat the flip'in queen of England.

I couldn't believe it. She made eye contact with me and nearly putting my mouth on the window glass I yelled, "Hey Queen Elizabeth, Jesus loves you! As guards began to pour out of cars to beat up the foreigner that was yelling at their monarch, the traffic began to move and off she went.

Watching them drive away, I held my wife's hand and muttered, "That was the Queen, Leanna. I just got to preach to the Queen."

A short sermon yes, but it was the best I could come up with for the time I had to put it together. You see, my obedience in going to the orphanage in Uganda placed me on the street corner in England. I thought about it all the way from London to Entebbe.

SOMETHING TO SIP ON

This week's sip from the Master's cup perks something like this; You will only do the great things God has called you to do if you are willing to be the person He has called you to be. Your character and your destiny go hand in hand. Your submission to the Lord in everyday life lands you in the right place at the right time for the right miracle to happen. Gods word to us truly is directing us to much greater things.

Your word is a lamp to my feet and a light for my path. Psalms 119:105

NOTES AND QUOTES : _____
_____
_____
_____
_____
_____
_____
_____

"Be sure you put your feet in the right place, then stand firm." - Abraham Lincoln: 16th President of the United States of America

"The two most important requirements for major success are: first, being in the right place at the right time, and second, doing something about it." -Ray Kroc : Founder of McDonalds

OVERCOMING IN THE DAY THE MUSIC DIES

On October 7th, 1995 Waylon Jennings returned to Clear Lake Iowa the same way he left 36 years before - by bus. More than 2,000 fans packed the Surf Ballroom to see a world famous performer, initially made famous by not being on the plane that killed Buddy Holly, Ritchie Valens and the Big Bopper. It was something that Waylon had avoided doing for more than three decades.

It seems that planes and musicians don't mix very well. The Freebird went down and killed most of the Lynard Skynard band. Patsy Cline, Hawkshaw Hawkins, Otis Redding, Jim Croce, Ricky Nelson and Stevie Ray Vaughn were all stars that fell from the sky. But the really big one that made the biggest impact was only a four-seater and one of those seats had belonged to Waylon Jennings.

The Big Bopper had the flu and he asked Waylon if he could have his place on the little plane because he couldn't sleep on the bus. Waylon being the low man on the totem pole agreed and so they sent him off to buy some hotdogs. When he got back, Buddy Holly was sitting in a chair, leaned back against the wall and grinning from ear to ear.

'So I hear you're not going with us on the plane tonight?" he said as Waylon handed him a hotdog.

"Well, I hope your ol' bus freezes up. It's 40-below out there and you're gonna get awful cold." So Waylon turned to him and said the last words he would ever say to his close friend,

"Well, I hope your ol' plane crashes."

The next day Waylon found out the same way the rest of the world did. The tour group left him stranded in Wisconsin and he had no way to get home or even go to the funeral. He spent several days sitting in a diner looking out at the cold hard winter and wondering what he was going to do. It was a devastating loss that shook every fiber of who he was.

THAT'LL BE THE DAY

So In 1995, Jennings returned to the Surf Ballroom, an authentic country legend and performer. He walked out onto the stage in his old age and long hair, remembering his youth and crew cut from 1959. The music was different and so was he. It was a big deal.

"The last time I was here I stood right over there," he said to the crowd on the night of his return, pointing to the left side of the stage. Jennings asked for the audience lights to be turned on, and the people cheered.

"I recognize this place and I recognize backstage. The last time I saw Buddy, he was leaning against the wall, thinking. Buddy did a lot of that."

"This is kind of a special night for me," Jennings said. "I lost some great friends that night. You should have known Buddy, The Big Bopper, and Ritchie Valens. They were great. That's all I'm going to say about that," he said, as he broke out into "Me and Bobby McGee."

That concert was more than a performance by a musician; it was about a man coming back to face one of the most tragic events of his life.

TRUE LOVE WAYS

What I really like about this story is that Waylon went back to the Surf Ballroom not as a victim, but as an overcomer. It hadn't been easy but somehow he went from a struggling bass player that lost a career in one tragic night to a country music legend that everybody wanted a piece of. He went back to that place but not as the person he used to be and that is the difference between his and a lot of other people's stories.

I don't know if Waylon was a Christian but these are the kinds of stories attached to victorious Christian people. I think God will eventually lead us back to those places where we were once defeated and have us stand there as the bad motor scooter He has made us to be. He makes us grow up. There is a healing for Christians I think that only comes from our journey in Christ where God will have us make friends with those terrible things that used to haunt us.

Not because we have to but because we have become so confident in who we are as victorious people, we can go through those places without being victimized.

As it is written, "For thy sake we are killed all the day long; we are accounted as sheep for the slaughter. Nay, in all these things we are more than conquerors through him that loved us." Romans 8:36 & 37

NOTES AND QUOTES

"Instead of weeping when a tragedy occurs in a songbird's life, it sings away its grief. I believe we could well follow the pattern of our feathered friends." -WILLIAM SHAKESPEARE: ENGLISH POET, PLAYWRIGHT AND ACTOR

The Brewer with Texas country artist Jeff Grossman.

THE SUMMER OF '69

The year was 1969. I was three years old and not really concerned with what was going on around me, except for wherever my blanket and binky was. While I wasn't really aware of it then, the summer of '69 was a world changing season.

At the time when my world was mostly about trying to decide if I liked green beans, others were concerned with some of the following events which happened that year.

The Charles Manson Murders took place. Woodstock and the Hippies were in full swing. The Vietnam War was raging. The Beetles played together for the last time. Richard Nixon was sworn in as president. Yassar Arafat became president of the PLO.

Golda Mier became the Israeli Prime Minister. Sesame Street came on the TV, and I found new friends. Sirhan Sirhan was convicted of the assassination of Robert Kennedy.

There was one more major event that happened that year. Yes I got potty trained…..well, for the most part. Sometimes I still have issues when I get excited.

Actually this year marks the 40th anniversary of a very major event - man's first landing on the moon!

ONE SMALL STEP FOR MAN

On July 16th, 1969 at 13:32 EDT, a three man crew with each one having two missions under their belt, soared with wings of eagles past the shackles of gravity to another place. It just happens that the lunar module was actually named Eagle.

In past confessions of this highly-caffeinated Christian, I have admitted that The Brewer does not like heights. I get a nose bleed when I put on my ropers and when I think about what these guys went through to leave our atmosphere, it blows my mind.

With the computer technology of a modern wrist watch, these three astronauts went so far and so high. I can't help but raise my cup to them.

Neil Armstrong was the Commander; Buzz Aldrin was the Lunar Module Pilot, and Michael Collins commanded the module. On July 20th, the Lunar Module piloted by Aldrin started its descent from Columbia. At 8:17 UTC (Coordinated Universal Time, same as Greenwich Mean Time), placed its lunar legs on the surface of the moon.

Neil Armstrong said "Houston, Tranquility Base here. The Eagle has landed". And with those eight words being spoken, a new era of space exploration began. It is interesting to note that the number eight in the Bible stands for "New Beginnings".

A little known fact about Buzz Aldrin is that he was a Christian. Approximately two and a half hours after the moon walk, he broadcasted to Houston that he would like to take the opportunity to ask everyone who was listening to contemplate the event which just happened and give thanks in their own way. He then took communion, there on the moon, and gave God thanks, which was his way. This communion kit is in the possession of the Webster Presbyterian Church in Webster, Texas where Aldrin was an elder.

ONE GIANT LEAP OF FAITH

Two thousand years ago, there was a man who left His footprints in the dust of planet earth. Instead of leaving the earth to the heavens, He left Heaven for earth. His impact upon this world is felt today in the four corners of the world.

There are millions who walk in his footprints. As Buzz Aldrin had communion in the heavens, this man had communion with his band of believers on this earth. As surely as Apollo 11 made history 40 years ago, this man made history 2000 years ago.

Man has vowed to return to the moon. This man that I'm talking about, has vowed He will also return and sooner than you think. His name is Jesus. His mission was divine. His goal was accomplished, and his vow to return will be fulfilled.

We may not be able to walk in the footprints of Neil Armstrong and Buzz Aldrin, but we can certainly walk in the footprints of Jesus. He has already cleared the minefields of life for all of us. All we need do is step where He steps….one step at a time

The steps of a good man are ordered by the Lord, And He delights in his way. Psalms 37:23

NOTES AND QUOTES

_____
_____
_____
_____
_____
_____

"Take the first step in faith. You don't have to see the whole staircase, just take the first step."

-Martin Luther King, Jr. : American pastor, activist, humanitarian, and leader in the Civil Rights Movement.

WHO'S THE GREATEST?

When it comes to boxing, most would agree that Cassias Clay, also known to the world over as Muhammad Ali, is the greatest heavy weight boxer—ever.

The Muhammad Ali of the 60's was certainly the fastest heavyweight ever. In the May 5, 1969, issue of Sports Illustrated, they measured his jab with an omegascope. That jab could smash a balsa board 16.5 inches away in 19/100 of a second. It actually covered the distance in 4/100 of a second, which is also the blink of an eye.

"He has no business being as fast as he is. I never saw that right hand," said Bob Foster, the world light heavyweight champion, after his fight with Ali.

Author John Durant described Ali as having "lightning fast hands and a pair of legs that moved around the ring like a ballet dancer. He would float just out of range with his hands dangling at his side as if to taunt his opponent.

'I am the greatest! I told the world, I am the greatest. You're going to go down. Can't stop it. You can't stop it. Here it comes,' he would say just before sticking a lighting fast jab and an unstoppable hook."

I think about people who are perceived as the best at what they do: Nolan Ryan, Elvis, John Wayne, Ted Williams, Stevie Ray Vaughn, Chuck Yaeger, Alexander...what was the rest of his title? Anyway, there is something to be said about the cream of the crop and something that reminds of me of the Kingdom of God.

THE FIGHT FOR GREATNESS

Anyone who begins to hang out with Jesus, no matter what kind of history they have, begins to contemplate their own untapped greatness. After a while in His presence, you become willing to fight for it. The dirty dozen whom Jesus assembled, were men of no notoriety before Jesus joined them. Yet, there was something about His presence that made them all feel like they were God's favorite and could do anything.

Luke 9:46
Then there arose a reasoning among them, which of them should be greatest.

Luke 22:24
And there was also a strife among them, which of them should be accounted the greatest.

Matthew 18:1
At the same time came the disciples unto Jesus, saying, "Who is the greatest in the kingdom of heaven?"

Mark 9:34
But they held their peace: for by the way they had disputed among themselves, who should be the greatest.

Hanging around Jesus Christ, breathing His words of life and thinking his thoughts makes you want to fight for greatness. So why isn't there more of that?

Sadly, the Church is more famous for dregs than for the best wine at the marriage supper. Here in the bible noose of the southern United States, we church leaders have been more about shouting, "You had better not," rather than, "Go forth." So we settle and we settle for something that once was, rather than fight for what could be.

Our fight for greatness gets replaced with a fight for preserving history, and that is where it really gets ugly. Whatever used to be a long time ago, religion likes to call that godliness. We must resist the Amish-like temptation to canonize an era and instead tap into how God is moving today. Just like the Pharisees and Scribes in Jesus' day, we become so familiar with an old move of God, we have no grid for a new move of God and our lack of pursuit for upgrade causes us to miss our day of visitation.

Religion and the Law always require what we can not pay and makes us failures, but the Grace of God always enables us to be and to do what was impossible before Jesus entered the picture. Grace, you gotta love it!

So, The Brewer herby informs you that it is my humble opinion that I am God's favorite and can do anything. I am also here to tell you that the bug for better is contagious. Once you hang around Jesus, you can argue with me over who is the coolest cat alive. Jesus has a funny way of empowering us all to believe Him for the greatest.

And now these three remain: faith, hope and love. But the greatest of these is love. 1 Corinthians 13:13

NOTES AND QUOTES

_____
_____
_____
_____

"Keep away from people who try to belittle your ambitions. Small people always do that, but the really great make you feel that you, too, can become great." – Mark Twain : American author and humorist

"Great spirits have always encountered violent opposition from mediocre minds." – Albert Einstein : theoretical physicist

PEOPLE WORTH REMEMBERING

The childhood years of Seth Ricketts was filled with G.I. Joes and Army men. He wanted to be a soldier as a little bitty guy and purposely never grew out of it. When he was only nine, Seth looked through the Yellow Pages to find a recruiter and made a phone call all by his big self.

"He wanted to be in the military since he was nine years old and had been talking to a recruiter," said his father, Bill Ricketts.

Seth grew up and then in 2001, all of America scrambled to find a TV set. We watched in horror as thousands of our country men were forced to jump to their deaths and even more climbed the narrow stair way to theirs. Muslim terrorists attacked the United States on 9-11 and Seth joined the Army on September 12th. Destiny called and true to form, Seth stepped up and stepped in. It was no surprise to Bill.

"He said he was going to protect his country and to keep that kind of stuff from happening to his family. He would rather take the fight to their soil." Bill proudly stated about his son.

But then there was Rosie. The love of his life was also proud of her soldier man and for the next nine years she would faithfully stand by him and for him as he completed three tours of duty in Iraq and two in Afghanistan. They had two kids together, 3-year-old Aiden and 10-month-old Cullen. Rosie is pregnant now with their third child, due this summer and his fifth tour of duty almost complete. So Seth agreed it was finally time to come home. He had been there for the births of his first two children, but deployed soon afterward. This time, he was looking forward to being home during the first part of his child's life.

So last week, there was the usual presentation of medals and accolades you would expect for such a warrior. They include the Army Commendation Medal, the Afghanistan Campaign Medal and the Iraqi Campaign Medal.

His platoon leader gave testimony to his values, dedication, and love like no other for his family and country. The home town newspaper ran a front page story on Seth and even his old school teachers chimed in on how proud they all are of him. But the newspaper headlines didn't say Seth had come home, -it said he would not. He was killed Saturday in Bala Murghab, Afghanistan while fighting with the 82nd airborne.

"He was an exemplary soldier and the men that were under him praised his work and his leadership," the soldier's father said. "He put his men before his own life. That's just who he was."

For as long as there has been anything worth keeping, protecting and achieving there have been wars. And as long as there have been wars there have been wives and parents and children who have received medals instead of the person they were hoping would come home.

MEMORIAL DAY

This week's sip from the Master's cup comes brewed with a grateful tear. I am so appreciative of the selflessness and commitment of our Armed forces. I am also heartbroken for the parents and the families of those who are truly grieving over the death of a warrior who fell in battle.

I think we Christians, should make a prayerful proclamation on behalf of every family hurting over this issue. I also think we should be ready to extend a hand or give a hug to those who need it. If you are hurting over the death of a soldier, please know that

I said a prayer for you today. On behalf of all readers and on behalf of the Troy Brewer family and my friends at Open Door, Thank you, we love you. May you know the peace that passes understanding and the greatest Peace maker of all, Jesus.

John 15:13 Greater love has no one than this, that he lay down his life for his friends.

NOTES AND QUOTES

_____
_____
_____
_____
_____
_____
_____
_____
_____
_____
_____
_____
_____
_____
_____

"Heroes are made by the paths they choose, not the powers they are graced with." – Brodi Ashton : American Novelist

"My own heroes are the dreamers, those men and women who tried to make the world a better place than when they found it, whether in small ways or great ones. Some succeeded, some failed, most had mixed results... but it is the effort that's heroic, as I see it. Win or lose, I admire those who fight the good fight." – George R.R. Martin

THE LIFE AND TIMES OF LARRY NORMAN

In 1947 the Normans gave birth to a bouncing baby boy they named Larry. Corpus Christi, Texas was a hard place to live so they moved to an apartment in the Haight-Ashbury District in San Francisco.

Though Born a Texan, Larry Norman was destined to be a Hippy.

As a teenager, he joined a band called People which in 1966 was offered a contract by Capitol Records. Though outwardly Christian, People would open for such secular giants of that era as the Doors, the Grateful Dead, Janis Joplin, and the Byrds. That's why Larry made such a big difference and it's also where the controversy was.

The solo career that followed was an adventurous dive into uncharted territory that Larry was perfectly built for. Throughout most of the 1970s, He was in the unique position of being too religious for rock-n-rollers, and too rockish for the church. It's for that reason Larry Norman got the attention of millions and gained influence over untold numbers who break out into their own Christian music or be openly Christian though in secular fields.

He was always under constant criticism by non- Christians wanting him to drop his faith and terrible protest by the conservative church wanting him to drop his music and cut his hair. Larry just kept on strumming his guitar and churning out songs.

BUMPS AND BRUISES

In 1978, while returning from a tour of Asia and the Middle East, he was injured in a plane crash on the taxiway at LAX.

Part of the overhead column dropped on his head, causing brain damage. It took him a while to recover but he kept taking his Christianity into non-Christian cultures.

Ten years later he was given a state-sponsored series of concerts in the USSR. While he was there, he was arrested, interrogated, poisoned and beaten by the KGB. Something he never really recovered from and something that didn't help his brain injury at all. When president Reagan found out, he invited Larry to perform at the white house.

Larry was a missionary in the truest since of the word. He just was so far outside of the box of traditional church most church leaders didn't know what to think about him.

ENTER THE BREWER

1989 saw the release of Stranded In Babylon, which was hailed by European critics as one of the best albums of the decade. It was barely noticed at all in the U.S.A. but it sure caught my attention. I enter this picture briefly, as a twenty two year old Christian musician playing for and being managed by a guy named Scotty Mckay. Scotty was friends with Larry Norman and when Larry came to Dallas, my band opened for him.

I never became great friends with Larry Norman but I did stay up till four in the morning jamming with him one night. I can honestly tell you I shared the same stage and sat in the same booth at an IHOP with Larry. It's one of my favorite memories.

Often regarded as the "father of Christian rock", Larry was inducted into the Gospel Music Association's Hall of Fame in 2001. We knew it was inevitable but none the less relieved that he was honored for his contribution. Time Magazine called Larry "The top solo artist in his field." Billboard Magazine is quoted as saying "The most important songwriter since Paul Simon."

Bob Dylan, Pete Townshend, Bono from U2, Van Morrison and John Cougar Mellencamp are just a few people that claim Larry influenced them greatly. You can add The Brewer to that list for what it's worth.

I woke up this morning thinking I would get a lot done but when I read Larry Norman had died, I knew I would be pounding away a tribute. Though, I am about as far away from being a hippy as one can be, Larry touched my life as he did millions of others. In my humble opinion the world is a lesser place without him.

Just before he died He dictated the following message.

"I feel like a prize in a box of cracker jacks with God's hand reaching down to pick me up. I have been under medical care for months. My wounds are getting bigger. I have trouble breathing. I am ready to fly home."

"My brother Charles is right, I won't be here much longer. I can't do anything about it. My heart is too weak. I want to say goodbye to everyone…I'd like to push back the darkness with my bravest effort….There will be a funeral posted here on the website, in case some of you want to attend. We are not sure of the date when I will die."

"Goodbye, farewell, we'll meet again
Somewhere beyond the sky.
I pray that you will stay with God.
Goodbye, my friends, goodbye.
Larry"

Thanks for being different Larry and thanks for making a difference. I really look forward to meeting you again, sir.

Revelation 21:4 He will wipe away every tear from their eyes, and death shall be no more, neither shall there be mourning, nor crying, nor pain anymore, for the former things have passed away."

NOTES AND QUOTES

_____
_____
_____
_____
_____
_____
_____
_____
_____
_____
_____
_____
_____
_____
_____

"Here's to the crazy ones. The misfits. The rebels. The trouble-makers. The round pegs in the square holes. The ones who see things differently. They're not fond of rules. And they have no respect for the status quo. You can quote them, disagree with them, glorify or vilify them. About the only thing you can't do is ignore them. Because they change things. They push the human race forward. And while some may see them as the crazy ones, we see genius. Because the people who are crazy enough to think they can change the world, are the ones who do."

– Apple INC : American multinational corporation, that designs & sells consumer electronics, computer software and personal computers.

The Brewer and a Hindu Priest at a water well in India 2012.

ISABELLA

Her name is Isabella. I saw her for the first time several years ago. We will both be forty two this winter. Past that, there's not much in common. Though we grew up on the same planet, during the same time, we have lived in two completely different worlds.

When I was eighteen, I drove a 1971, Ford truck named "Ned Pepper" after the bad guy from True grit. It was a shining time for me, full of music, friends, high school graduations and hope for the future. That same year, when Isabella was eighteen, her family sold her to the trash dump in Matamoros Mexico.

ACROSS THE RIVER

The search for a better life had brought Isabella's family to the border. They had heard there were jobs that couldn't be found in the mountains of Southern Mexico. They didn't find jobs but found hardship and predators that prey on desperate people.

After spending some time without a home, they were offered a piece of property with no money down, where they could build some kind of a house from things found at the nearby dump. What seemed like a good opportunity was actually a trap. Because they didn't understand how interest works, it wasn't long before they couldn't make the payment.

The terrible ultimatum demanded by these Mafioso loan sharks is that your wife and daughters can either sell their bodies as prostitutes or the whole family can work in the trash dump. Of course they are promised they will be able to pay off the debt, and of course they are never able to. Years go by, people lose hope and slavery goes on within a few hours drive of where you are reading this now.

A CROSS TO BEAR

I don't know all the details but Isabella became property of the dump the same year I was eating ice cream at the Dairy Queen in Joshua. She paid the price for her family at the age of 18 and her family went back to the village. She was 36 now but looked much older, emotionally disturbed and a little bit crazy. Isabella had spent every day of her last 18 years in untold hardship and every night in unspeakable darkness.

Her "boss" was there that first day we met her. He sat in the truck watching her and some twenty others mine through the filth for anything of value.

Through several local people, we were told her story and we approached her about the possibility of freedom. I asked if it was possible to pay her debt and set her free. She didn't say anything she just smiled and pointed to the guy in the truck. A local Pastor hacked out a price for this human being and all of us on the team collected our money. Out of the 10 of us we were able to muster $631.00. He took the money, went and had a talk with her and drove off to parts unknown.

We set Isabella free that day. Free to find her family. Free to live wherever she wanted, however she wanted. At that moment I felt like one of the most privileged people who ever lived. It was a good day.

CROSSING BACK OVER

I visit the dumps there several times a year, so four years later it wasn't out of the ordinary for us to be there again. When we topped the hill with our truckload of food and clothes, I thought I recognized her. There in the trash she was collecting cardboard. Isabella was back. My heart sank.

It wasn't the loan shark or another con. She was there working on her own free will. "Forgive me", she said to our team, "I don't know how to live out there I only know this place." She looked for any sign of mercy and all I could do was hug her and tell her it was ok.

Every time I go there I see her now. She runs to the truck before we can even get out and we are always happy to share a day together. In fact we put special things aside for her and her family. I got to put brand new shoes on her little boy's feet last week and my wife paid to put all of her kids through another year of school.

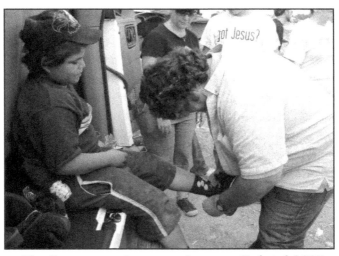

- The Brewer putting new shoes on Gabriel 2007.

Yes, I'm disappointed she chose to stay in the dump, but she is still very precious to the Brewer bunch. I just don't think Isabella could see herself outside of that terrible place. Because of her self-identity, the dump still has her. I wish she could see herself like we see her because we think she's awesome.

I see all of us in Isabella. Christ has set us free and so many times we choose to go back to the trash. It's hard to see yourself as clean and set free when on the inside you feel filthy and tied up. That is why it's so important to believe the truth especially when it comes to identity. When we believe a lie we empower the liar and that's just a shame. May we all learn to see ourselves a little more like God really sees us.

And ye shall know the truth, and the truth shall make you free. John 8:32

- Isabella, with my son Benjamin.

POST NOTE: a few years after this column was printed, Isabella, moved out of the dump but continued to work there. Finally in 2009, we were no longer greeted by her. She had completely moved away!

I don't suppose I will ever see her on this side of heaven but I think about her all the time.

God used Isabella to teach me a lot about how redemption works. You can be completely set free and still not convinced of it.

I am convinced God understands the process and continues to love us in extraordinary ways even though we continue to run back to the trash dumps we have been redeemed from.

Sometimes it takes a while to make that transition.

NOTES AND QUOTES

_____
_____
_____
_____
_____
_____
_____
_____
_____
_____
_____
_____
_____

"Everybody is in a process. It's not that Jesus won't transform the lives of hurting people. The issue is will the church put up with people long enough to see them transformed without hurting them worse or stopping the process." -Troy Brewer : Twiddler of Thumbs. Amateur Yodeler. Competitive Ear Wiggler.

"If Jesus Christ was who He claimed to be, and He did die on a cross at a point of time in history, then, for all history past and all history future it is relevant because that is the very focal point for forgiveness and redemption."-Josh McDowell: Christian Apologist, Evangelist, and Writer.

TITANIC THOMPSON

A few weeks ago I wrote a story on the Titanic. If you didn't get a chance to read it, I would like to shamelessly plug the Brewer's website where you can go to our Blog and check the archives. It's FreshFromTheBrewer.com. Today's cup from this highly caffeinated Christian is about an all-together different Titanic. This Titanic wasn't a boat but a person.

Odds are you never have heard of Titanic Thompson, who sailed through life as the greatest poker playing, golf gambling, horseshoe hustling, skeet shooting, womanizing, rake-hell, con man of all time. That doesn't mean he didn't leave his mark.

Titanic Thompson was America's most famous gambler, card cheat, and sharp dressed man for decades. His celebrity status was so great, Houdini himself followed him trying to find his secrets to swindling people. Thompson was actually the model for Damon Runyon's character Sky Masterson in the Broadway play *Guys and Dolls*. Marlon Brando played his part in the movie.

It was only at Titanic's insistence that the writer called his gambling lead man by another name. Titanic was already more famous than he wanted to be. So Runyon christened his romantic lead, «Sky Masterson,» for the 'master' Titanic, whose 'sky's the limit' response was a sure thing whenever a bet was on the table.

His skills got him personally invited to a party by Al Capone and he had the guts to cheat Capone in a bet, which he did, and got away with it. He often played pool with Minnesota Fats. He was a professional golfer and actually good enough to shoot a 29 on the back nine at Fort Worth's Ridglea Country Club where he beat Byron Nelson by one stroke.

ALWAYS AN ANGLE

He was the Arizona State trapshooting champion four consecutive years. He was a quick draw pistoleer and somehow got away with at least five shootings and some say six in which all men were killed. It was said that he could throw a baseball from dead center field 400 feet to home plate without the aid of a bounce and he would challenge professional baseball players in throwing matches. One time, he challenged the horseshoe throwing world champion to a high stakes game and beat him out of $2000.

Titanic, who was naturally left-handed, played Golf just as well right-handed, and he would often hustle golfers by challenging them to a game where he would switch hands. But being good at golf was all about getting him into country clubs from coast to coast. Once inside, Titanic could always find rich men and take them for all they had in much more lucrative poker games. It paid a lot better than those tiny golf purses. This was way before Tiger Woods.

In 1972, Titanic as an old man, agreed to do a rare interview with Sports Illustrated. They offered to pay him a much-needed $5000 for the story. In the two weeks Bud Shrake spent with him putting it together, Titanic made a huge impression. Shrake wrote, "Ti's mind was so sharp that I am convinced if he was born in Princeton, N.J. instead of Nowhere, Ark. and went to an Ivy League college, he'd have spent his life giving advice to world leaders".

As a ladies man, he could just as easily talk a woman into loving him as he could talk a man into a bet. There was something about him people thought they could tame. He counted on that underestimation and used it frequently. Titanic married 5 times and all of them teenagers. When he died at the age of 81, his last wife of 19 years was 37. This guy was something else.

One of his abandoned offspring, Tommy Thomas, caught up with him in San Antonio at the age of nineteen. 1964 was a good year for Tommy and he rolled up into the driveway in a shiny jaguar. Always hoping to someday impress his dad, he himself was quite an accomplished card shark.

Over the next several years they paired up and racked in millions from unsuspecting wannabes. I know all this not just because of the books I've read on Titanic Thompson but because Tommy Thomas, Titanic's son, is a friend of mine.

Today, Tommy is a Preacher and has a TV show called How to Beat the Odds. I've been on his show a couple times and know for a fact it airs all over the world. One time, my wife and I were visiting our orphanage in Uganda and Tommy's show was airing and it just happened to be the show that I was on. It was a hoot to bring in the staff at the little hotel and all of us watched it together.

The one thing Tommy will tell you that he really wanted out of his dad was to hear the words, "I love you" In all those years, Titanic's pride wouldn't allow him to bless his boy with the affirmation he desperately needed. Finally, and literally the day before he died of a stroke, Ti Thompson put his arms around Tommy and said the magic words he had wanted to hear.

UNSINKABLE

What it always comes down to is whom you love and who loves you. For those of us that cling to Christianity, we know this to be true. Whatever exploits you've lived, good or bad, mean nothing the last few days in the old folks home. The only real legacy any of us have is a testimony of whom we have loved and who loved us.

Let it be said of the Brewer, that I loved God and God really loved this ol' knucklehead. If that's true (and I know it is) the love of God will outlast all of my history, no matter how titanic my sin may have been.

«And a voice from heaven said, 'This is my Son, whom I love; with him I am well pleased.» Matthew 3:17

NOTES AND QUOTES

_____
_____
_____
_____
_____
_____
_____
_____
_____
_____
_____
_____
_____
_____
_____
_____

"Your story is the greatest legacy that you will leave to your friends. It's the longest-lasting legacy you will leave to your heirs." – Steve Saint : Ecuadorian-born business entrepreneur, pilot, and author.

REFLECTIONS OF A LEMONHEAD

If you were a young man in your early twenties, and actually locked lips with Angelina Jolie, do you think you would know it? I know that seems like a ridiculous question, but after you scan through this story you might not think so. This week's cup from a highly caffeinated Christian comes freshly brewed with off the wall reflections on how easily we miss really big things.

EVAN ALMIGHTY

Fifteen years ago, Evan Dando headed up a band called the Lemonheads and gained wide recognition for its 1992 cover of "Mrs. Robinson." He was the good looking son of a fashion model and fit in well with the Hollywood A-list. He moved into a house owned by Johnny Depp. People magazine listed him as on one of the top 50 dishiest people, whatever that is. His album, It's a Shame about Ray took off, selling millions.

Dando saw his dreams come true and then, predictably, saw nothing but a blur. The fast lane of superstardom turned on him like an evil genie, and the next fifteen years were full of drugs, breakups, scandals, failures and disappointments.

Sometime around 2005, Evan emerged from his fog and started recording with the Lemonheads again. It was a bonafied comeback, and Evan's heart began to come back to life. His new success sparked a string of live performances and interviews, and that's when I caught his story in an American Airlines magazine.

When I got back to the house, I looked him up on the World Wide Waste of time and saw this side note in an interview. He said recently someone had asked him if Angelina Jolie was a good kisser, and he replied, "You would have to ask Brad Pitt". The interviewer informed him that Angelina was seen kissing him in one of his music videos. He went back to watch it, and sure enough—he had spent an entire afternoon in 1992 filming kissing scenes with the now famous movie star—and didn't even remember it.

PUCKER UP

The blur and the busyness of our fast-paced lives can make us miss a lot of things. Extraordinary things. I think the condition of our heart determines a lot of what we do and do not see in the lives around us. Evan was so miserable with the life he was living; he completely missed the experience of what was right in front of him. All of us have been Evan at one time or another. Many of us are doomed to forever be lemonheads.

Not me. I believe in curses and blessings, and a common curse is when somebody misses their marriage because they want to be single, or they miss single life because they want to be married. A lot of people hate getting up in the morning because they want to be retired and then hate retirement because they want to go back to work.

Deuteronomy 28 defines this internal affliction in verse 67:

In the morning you shall say, Would that it were evening! And at evening you shall say, would that it were morning! --Because of the anxiety and dread of your [minds and] hearts…

You don't have to have a Caribbean witch shake a dead rooster at you. All you gotta do is miss the moment. This curse is about the inability to see and enjoy the right now of life. A humble heart and a right mind will cause you to see the things that really matter when you are supposed to see them.

As you get about in your busy day, I encourage you to learn to be happy with what you already have. Don't be a lemonhead. Consider where you are with a grateful heart and you just might find you are a lot better off than you give God credit for.

NOTES AND QUOTES _____

_____
_____
_____
_____
_____
_____
_____
_____
_____
_____
_____
_____
_____
_____
_____
_____
_____

"We seem to live in a world where forgetting and oblivion are an industry in themselves and very, very few people are remotely interested or aware of their own recent history, much less their neighbors'. I tend to think we are what we remember, what we know. The less we remember, the less we know about ourselves, the less we are. " – Carlos Ruiz Zafón : Spanish novelist

"Don't limit yourself. Many people limit themselves to what they think they can do. You can go as far as your mind lets you. What you believe, remember, you can achieve." – Mary Kay Ash: American businesswoman

The Brewers Making out at the Taj Mahal 2013.

A TRIBUTE TO PAULA

Many of you already know that my long time friend and personal secretary, Paula Ledbetter, died in her sleep last Friday morning. She was only 37 years old but she made 100 years worth of difference in our lives and in the world she lived in. Today's sip from the carpenter's cup is mixed with a bitter sweet tear or two, I hope you'll continue sipping as I honor my friend and glorify the Lord.

If you have ever been to one of our food outreaches, church services or music concerts, you have seen Paula. It has been the habit of my wife and I, not to go very far without her because she helped us to do everything.

Paula cleaned the church, answered the phones, cut every ones hair for free, organized our big events, structured the deacons ministry, took food to folks that couldn't come to get it, arranged all of my evangelical meetings, helped me keep track of my newspaper columns, watch our kids, made me coffee and worked hard on all our missions trips.

I am convinced that if you look up the word "selfless" or possibly "loyal" or may be even "dedicated" in the dictionary, you will see Paula's smiling face right beside it. We will miss her in such an incredible way because she made such a big difference in so many arenas.

Paula was an outstanding wife to her wonderful husband, John Ledbetter. She was a joy for John to come home to and their 18 year marriage was blessed abundantly. She selflessly served the love of her life in every way she could, especially in prayer and service. She stood by John and for John in all she did every day of the week.

Paula's skill as a mother is incredibly evident through the life of her three teenage boys. All of them are fine young men with a strong balance of fun nature and hard dedication when they have to have it. She was an incredible mother to her kids and I know that those boys will marry fine women someday because they have seen the perfect model of what a wife and mother should look like.

Paula was a joy to have as a daughter in law to Charlie and Jerri Ledbetter. She was an incredible friend to my wife and a devoted church secretary to Open Door.

If you missed Paula's funeral service, you missed one of the greatest send offs I have ever had the privilege of being a part of. Over 600 people tried to cram into a room that only held 250 and we literally applauded Paula's life and the Lord she loved so much.

It was easy to mark the qualities that made Paula so special. It was effortless to put together a sermon that praised God and honored Paula because she lived such an honorable life. It was simple to point out what a difference she made when you have hundreds of people packed in a room and hundreds more outside that can't get in because they all loved Paula so much.

I am telling you that God moved in such a powerful way at her funeral I almost got saved again myself! In all seriousness, from what I have been able to gather, 17 people dedicated their hearts to the Lord that day. It was an incredible moment of victory in a time when most are completely defeated.

That was true to form for Paula. She was always making something wonderful out of something bad. Weather it was a gourmet meal out of macaroni and leftovers or somebody's nasty feet into a pedicure, she knew how to turn bad things into good things.

This is the mark of people that truly follow Jesus Christ. Where there is darkness there is light. Wear there is failure there is hope. Where there is pain there is healing. And finally where there is death there is victory.

In Luke 4:16 Jesus said;

"The Spirit of the Lord is on me, because he has anointed me to preach good news to the poor, to bind up the brokenhearted, to comfort all who mourn, and provide for those who grieve, to bestow on them a crown of beauty instead of ashes, the oil of gladness instead of a spirit of despair."

We are all heartbroken at the death of our sister but by no means are we defeated. I mean, Paula was not defeated so why should we be? The fact of the matter is Paula's story doesn't end there and I thank God it doesn't. It may be a fact that Paula lost a long time battle last Friday but I know it's the Truth that she did not lose the war. She has victory against death and it was won for her on a battle field 2000 years ago by a champion named Jesus Christ.

I wonder if I could stand at your funeral and declare certain victory for you the same way I did for Paula. I wonder if I could stand and speak of your unwavering faith, your selfless service and your dedication to the things that really matter. Or I wonder if your funeral would be a sad, boring sermon where the best thing I could say for you is that you liked to play golf or you had joined the union at work or maybe loved your dog or your cat.

The truth is that if your life is all about you and how you can advance your own personal agenda, the world will not be worse off without you. However, if you have the same testimony that Paula has, and you have spent your life serving God and serving those around you, we will always have good reason to celebrate your life and to truly mourn your death. It is when you consider how short life really is, you begin to get in a hurry to take care of the things that really do matter.

Teach us, oh Lord, to number our days that we may apply our hearts unto wisdom.

Psalms 90:12

Good bye for now my friend. I am proud of you, Paula and I will see you on the great day!

POST COLUMN UPDATE

At the time that Paula died, I was in Costa Rica about to visit an orphanage I had never ventured to. Paula died suddenly and unexpectedly in her sleep from complications of a seizure. None of us could have imagined such a thing and it was literally a miracle that got me back to the states in time to do her funeral.

Paula had four men in her life. Her husband John and her three young teenage boys. I watched John remain a faithful follower of Jesus, overcome when he knew how to and just hold on when he didn't. I have really marveled at him through the years. Certainly changed from Paula's absence but extremely built up from the years she was with him.

He didn't twist off or freak out, he just quietly stepped through the incredible pain of his loss and did all he could to be a blessing to his boys and faithful to the Lord. I know it has not been easy for him but he makes it look easy and for that, he will always have my great respect.

I got to see her boys grow up into men and what fine men they are. All of them just incredible. Her oldest son, JC, married my youngest daughter in what was a dream come true for Paula.

When they were just babies, Paula would tell us, "You know they are going to get married someday. You watch, God told me they are going to get married someday."

I could not be more happy that Paula's prophecy came true. She didn't have to live past 37 to see the event, even though Rhema and JC got married many years after she died. Paula saw a lot of things because her heart was full of light. So is her legacy.

Nearly a decade has passed and I haven't been back to Costa Rica -until now. Mostly because I just wanted to avoid this place, I guess. But I came back here to finish a book on columns she had created.

She was the one who forced me to write my very first one, had it put in the paper and really encouraged me in becoming a writer. Costa Rica is even more beautiful than I remember it to be.

NOTES AND QUOTES

_____

_____

_____

_____

_____

_____

_____

_____

_____

_____

"I was standing in our dining-room thinking of nothing in particular, when a cablegram was put into my hand. It said, 'Susy was peacefully released today.' It is one of the mysteries of our nature that a man, all unprepared, can receive a thunder-stroke like that and live." – Mark Twain

GETTING THE LEAD OUT OF BEING LED

Audie Murphy

On October the 13th of 1971, the Honorable Olin Teague of Texas declared the following statement to his fellow members of congress to be put in the congressional record forever.

"Mr. Speaker, during World War II, Audie Murphy, the son of a Texas tenant farmer was awarded 24 citations for his battlefield deeds including the Medal of Honor and a battlefield commission as a 2nd Lieutenant.

In January 1945, the infantry company which Lieutenant Murphy commanded in eastern France was besieged by six German tanks. Lieutenant Murphy ordered his men to withdraw to prepared positions in the woods, while he remained forward at his command post and continued to give fire directions to the artillery by telephone. Behind him, to his right, one of our tank destroyers received a direct hit and began to burn. Its crew withdrew to the woods.

Lieutenant Murphy continued to direct artillery fire which killed large numbers of advancing enemy infantry. With the enemy tanks abreast of his position, Lieutenant Murphy climbed on the burning tank destroyer, which was in danger of blowing up at any moment, and employed its 50 caliber machine gun against the enemy. He was alone and exposed to German fire from three sides, but his deadly fire killed dozens of Germans and caused the attack to waiver. The enemy tanks, losing infantry support, began to fall back. For an hour the Germans tried every available weapon to eliminate Lieutenant Murphy, but he continued to hold his position and wiped out a squad which was trying to creep unnoticed on his right flank.

Germans reached as close as 10 yards, only to be mowed down by his fire. He received a leg wound, but ignored it and continued the single handed fight until his ammunition was exhausted. He then made his way to his company, refused medical attention, and organized the company in a counterattack which forced the Germans to withdraw. Lieutenant Murphy's indomitable courage and his refusal to give an inch of ground saved his Company from possible encirclement and destruction, and enabled it to hold the woods which had been the enemy's objective."

Infantryman Tony V. Abramski, who witnessed the brave actions of Lieutenant Murphy said later - 'The fight that Lieutenant Murphy put was the greatest display of guts and courage I have ever seen. There is only one in a million who would be willing to stand up on a burning vehicle, loaded with explosives around 250 raging Krauts for an hour and do all of that when he was wounded.'

After having been wounded three times in later combat activity, young Audie Murphy returned home to a Nation eager to honor its war heroes. He wanted to stay in the Army and become a career soldier but was turned down after being classified 50 percent disabled because of his war wounds."

This caffeinated Christian has read all of the accounts of what Audie Murphy did in that one small sliver of time that defined his entire life. It is truly amazing. When I think about that wounded, teenage Texan climbing on top of that burning vehicle and pointing that 50 caliber towards the enemy and surviving in heavy combat for more than an hour, I think that there was a godly set-up involved.

God knows you better than you know you. He knows how you will react not only to a certain situation but in fact to any given situation. He knows where you will succeed and he knows where you will fail. God almighty knew that most people would fail in that situation but he trusted Audie with it any way.

I believe there are some situations, which you don't have a clue about, that if you are at the right place at the right time and if the environment is just right you will make the right decision, you will prosper, prevail, and flourish and it'll be great. God will be glorified, your testimony will remain intact and you will be blessed.

But there are some situations and things that if you faced them you would fail miserably and you would succumb to defeat in such a way that you would be an embarrassment to your family and a reproach to your Creator.

One of the great things about walking with the Lord is that the longer you walk with Him, the more you find yourself being an overcomer in situations and in circumstances that you never thought possible. The reason for that is because as we follow Him as Christians He promises to "Lead" us into better places. Part of that leading is into places where we will win and not loose. As you mature in Christ you find that your heart has been changed and you can deal with things you couldn't deal with before.

I am no Audie Murphy but I am victorious. I don't claim credit for it either. I am just a guy that has walked with Jesus long enough for him to be led into incredible places where the Krauts should have gotten me. He knows how to keep me out of places where I will mess up, so it's best I just let Him do the leading - even if it's onto a burning vehicle.

Romans 8:14 For as many as are led by the Spirit of God, they are the sons of God.

NOTES AND QUOTES

"Courage is resistance of fear, Mastery of fear. It is not the absence of fear." - Mark Twain

The Brewer and his famous prayer sword 2008.

TRIUMPHANT NAVIGATION

On July 17, 1938, pilot Douglas Corrigan took off from Brooklyn's Floyd Bennett Field as family and friends watched. He only carried with him two chocolate bars, two boxes of fig bars, a quart of water, and a U.S. map with the route from New York to California marked out. His goal was to fly non-stop.

Corrigan took off in his modified Curtiss Robin equipped with a big V8 engine. It was a foggy morning. He flew into the haze and disappeared.

Twenty-eight hours later he successfully landed but not in California, in Dublin, Ireland three thousand miles the opposite direction. He instantly became a national hero because it was a feat thought impossible at the time, but from that day forward he was known as Wrong Way Corrigan.

BEAD CRUMBS AND THE NORTH STAR

Some people have a knack for direction and some people are just naturally lost as a burp in a hurricane. The Brewer is one of those people that you could blind fold, turn me a round and I probably would be able to point out north once I quit being dizzy. I have heard it's an inner ear thing but there are those of us that just have a really good sense of bearing. I've always been like that. It reminds me of what Brian Keith said to Charlton Heston in the 1980 movie, The Mountain Men. "No, I never get lost. Fearsome confused for weeks at a time, but I never get lost."

It's very embarrassing for a guy like me to get lost. I don't know why but I'm always convinced I'll get to the right place and I tend to get mad at the road if it doesn't cooperate with me. If I do get lost, it's usually because I am talking on the cell phone. I miss exits and outright drive to wrong cities if I stay on the phone long enough. I have been known to hang up the phone look at where I'm driving and say, "How did I end up here?" That's scary.

GPS AND ON STAR

The same type thing happened to Commander George P. Ryanway before I ever drove to Dallas. On November 23, 1877 the last of the great steam naval ships, the USS Huron left port and headed south towards Cuba. The Captain represented the brightest of his day and he had actually taught navigation at West Point. Because of his education he ignored warning after warning of approaching storms confident that his compass and his knowledge could weather any storm. But what he didn't know was that there was a tiny 1-degree error in the ships compass and the further they headed south, the closer his ship would edge towards the reefs of the east coast. In fact, within 24 hours the Huron would sink just 200 yards off the coast of Virginia and 98 men would lose their lives to the waves and the current.

When the warning bells rang, the Captain saw the rocks of the reef directly ahead and there was no way they could stop in time. He commanded his men to brace themselves and his last recorded words were, "MY GOD, HOW DID WE GET HERE?"

THE BRIGHT AND MORNING STAR

Ryanway was lost because what he trusted wasn't true. I was lost because I was distracted and not paying attention. "Wrong way Corrigan" was lost because he was blind in the fog. Whatever the reason, this is not a good year for you to be lost. As a Christian, my prayer for you is that God would lead you, guide you and direct you into better places. I hope that through the Holy Spirit you could find clear definition, forward progression and head into a hopeful place with confidence.

I believe that if you've never really got what "the Jesus thing" is to those of us that call ourselves saved, you can personally seek Him and find Him for yourself. I also believe if you once had a walk with God and somehow fell out, Jesus wants you back. Out of all the things I have to struggle with, being lost is not one of them. It's the most precious gift anyone has ever given me because it was my greatest need. Man, am I ever a guy in desperate need of a Savior and how grateful I am to have Him!

Matthew 18:14
In the same way your Father in heaven is not willing that any of these little ones should be lost.

NOTES AND QUOTES

_____

_____

_____

_____

_____

_____

_____

_____

_____

_____

_____

"In this world, it is too common for people to search for someone to lose themselves in. But I am already lost. I will look for someone to find myself in." – C. JoyBell C.

SOMETIMES ON THE WAY TO A DREAM

YOU GET LOST...AND FIND A BETTER ONE

REFUSING TO LIVE LIKE A REFUGEE

OLD SALAMANDER

During the War of 1812, a ship called the Essex sailed to South America, where the precocious David Glasgow Farragut took a captured British ship into Santiago, Chile. His ship was defeated and sank after a cannon blast. He didn't much care for his ship going down but he sure loved the Navy.

49 years later at the start of the Civil War, Farragut was a 60 year old naval captain living in Virginia. A Southerner by birth, Farragut nonetheless pledged his allegiance to the Union and was given command of a heavy fleet. His orders were to open the Mississippi by taking New Orleans. When he did, he was made the first rear admiral in U.S. Navy history. He ran his ships into terrible cannon fire, survived and became known as «Old Salamander.» A naval term of endearment for the crusty admiral.

Sixteen months later, he took the last Confederate stronghold on the Gulf of Mexico in the Battle of Mobile Bay. Ready to end the battle, he charged the heavily guarded bay entrance even though it was loaded with mines, then known as torpedoes. When they spotted the deadly explosives, Farragut pointed his saber towards the enemy and cried "Damn the torpedoes! Full speed ahead!". The stuff of legends.

HEART BREAKERS

114 years later a Florida boy living in Los Angeles was trying to think of a good title for his latest recording project. It was not a good year for Tom Petty but things were about to get better. The pressure of the music business was getting to him. His Label ABC Records tried to sell his contract to MCA records without Tom and the heartbreakers even knowing about it. He was angry at the whole system. He was defiant. He decided to go forward anyway, refusing to be victimized. The band pushed forward

through everything that threatened them and recorded a classic which he titled "Damn the Torpedoes!"

It was in that kind of mood. A mood that said things might blow up but I'm going forward, that Tom and fellow heartbreaker Mike Campbell wrote a smash hit titled "Refugee." It's a song about refusing to lay in defeat and going full steam ahead.

"Somewhere, somehow somebody must have kicked you around some

Tell me why you wanna lay there and revel in your abandon.

Listen, it don't make no difference to me. Everybody's got to fight to be free

You see you don't have to live like a refugee."

SAFE HAVENS

A refugee is somebody that doesn't have a refuge. A sanctuary, a shelter. Refugees struggle to survive because they don't have a place of protection.

Miraculous survivor stories tend to have something in common, a place of refuge.

The Japanese businessman survived the Hiroshima blast because he was working in a bank vault. An Indonesian woman survived 5 days at sea after the tsunami carried her away from her family. She did so by clutching a palm tree in the Indian Ocean, eating the fruit and bark of the tree she held on to. Don't you just love a good survival story? So does God.

God knows the importance of refuge. He doesn't offer to build you one; He offers to be your refuge. In Psalms 57:1 David writes, Be merciful to me oh God. For my soul trusts in you: And in the shadow of your wings I will make my refuge.

Max Lucado, in his Thomas nelson book Facing your Giants, says it a lot better than I could. "Make God your refuge. Not your job, your spouse, your reputation, or your retirement account. Make God your refuge. Let him, not Saul, encircle you. Let Him be the ceiling that breaks the beating sun, the walls that stop the wind, the foundation on which you stand."

Tom petty says you don't have to live like a refugee. Jesus says come to me.

Proverbs 18:10 The name of the LORD is a strong tower: the righteous runneth into it, and is safe.

NOTES AND QUOTES

_____
_____
_____
_____
_____

"Strength doesn't come from what you can do. Strength comes from overcoming the things you once could not do."   Mark Bannister

"Ban, delete, shred, obliterate the words "I am not good enough."" -Karen Salmonsohn

John 16:33   I have said these things to you, that in me you may have peace. In the world you will have tribulation. But take heart; I have overcome the world."

1 John 5:4 For everyone who has been born of God overcomes the world. And this is the victory that has overcome the world— our faith.

A KNIGHT TO REMEMBER

My father in law, Ray Knight, had been going down hill for sometime but he told all of us he would do his best to live to see Christmas. Hospice wasn't so sure, but Ray insisted he would be there for the annual celebration and family get together.

He was bound and determined he knew exactly when he would be leaving Texas and entering Heaven.

"Sometime after Christmas and before the New year", Ray said smiling, like he always did.

There's a neat thing that happens in my wife's family where people tend to know when their days are done. Ray's Grandfather was one of those guys and probably the most pronounced with this gift.

Grandpa Knight was well in his nineties when he decided to build his church a new building. "It will take me about two years", he said, "and the first service we are going to have in it will be my funeral."

Just like he promised, he finished his building two years later. Now what happened next is legendary in his church and among our family. Grandpa Knight went home that day, called his son, put on a suit, and climbed into bed and died! The very first service was indeed his funeral service just like he prophesied.

His Grandson, my wife's dad, had some of that in him. When I walked into his room on Christmas day he was excited about having a very real white Christmas, A rare oddity in Texas. He was feeling good and in a great mood.

"Well, you did it Ray, you made it to Christmas like you said you would." I said, as I helped him sit up to eat. "You think you will make it to New Years?"

"No I'm not gonna be here for New Years." He said smiling.

"Come on Ray, you look great today, you look better than I do." and Ray never missed a beat, "I always look better than you do."

Later that night after we had all gone home, Ray went unconscious and passed away on the morning of the 27th. Like Babe Ruth calling his shot, Ray Knight hit it out the ballpark by knowing the right time.

All of us will cherish that white Christmas as Ray's last day with us. I especially appreciate the opportunity we had to say our goodbyes and to pray together. It is only fitting that I tell you what scripture he told my wife was his favorite on Christmas day. There is some wisdom in it for all of us.

So teach us to number our days, that we may apply our hearts unto wisdom» (Psalm 90:12).

The Brewer at Hadrian's wall in Northern England 2014.

CHAPTER TWO
TEXAS AND SOME OTHER HISTORY

To me a big part of my love for History is looking at it like a study of people. Even people I don't like can still be really interesting. Another big reason for my love of History is because my dad, Bill Brewer, is a bigger history nerd than I am.

His love for Texas History infected me at a very early age and I have had the privilege of visiting Texas revolutionary battlefields all of the state with him.

My very British friend, Phillip David Lloyd, laughs at the notion of Texas History and calls it an oxymoron because of our short time frame. I simply explained to him that what took Europeans several thousand years to make a dent, only took us a couple of decades. Texas is accelerated if nothing else.

My thoughts and spin on all things History tend to show me whole new scenes into the hearts of men and the heart of God. History to me, is really HIS-Story. Especially Texas History.

*THE BREWER ON THE DAY HE WAS THE OFFICIAL
PASTOR OVER THE STATE OF TEXAS.
APRIL 15TH 2013*

DECISIVE BATTLES

SAINTS AT SAN JACINTO

The Brewer is a sixth-generation Texan and dang proud of it. I have an ancestor, Henry Brewer who actually fought along-side Sam Houston at the Battle of San Jacinto.

I was there, if only in microscopic form and really glad (for my sake) that Henry Brewer was with Houston, instead of Travis at the Alamo.

San Jacinto is the decisive battle that won Texas her independence. To wrap your head around what a big deal it really is, it's important you read the inscription carved into the monument that stands on the battlefield today.

"Measured by its results, San Jacinto was one of the decisive battles of the world. The freedom of Texas from Mexico won here led to annexation and to the Mexican-American War, resulting in the acquisition by the United States of the states of Texas, New Mexico, Arizona, Nevada, California, Utah and parts of Colorado, Wyoming, Kansas and Oklahoma. Almost one-third of the present area of the American Nation, nearly a million square miles of territory, changed sovereignty."

In other words, there is a reason why people in Ft worth, Salt Lake, and Los Angeles don't have to live the lifestyle of our neighbors in Matamoras, Juarez and Tijuana. That reason is because of a handful of heroes, not even trained solders, who chose to oppose and defeat a dictator back in 1836.

THE FIGHT IS ON

Some battles are so strategically important that everything afterwards hinges upon the results of that single event. I wonder if those Texans knew how important that one single battle actually was. I know that HOUSTON did but I bet most of the others were trying to get through it.

I wonder if you know how important it is that you win the battles you are fighting. Unseen spiritual battles in brutal mental and emotional arenas you are choosing to oppose.

There is a lot more on the line for what you think then what you might think.

"For though we walk in the flesh, we do not war according to the flesh. For the weapons of our warfare are not carnal but mighty in God for pulling down strongholds, casting down arguments and every high thing that exalts itself against the knowledge of God, bringing every thought into captivity to the obedience of Christ" 2 Corinthians 10:3-5

Every Christian has to fight, in order to hang onto and possess the land, or to have victory with the territory God trusts us with. Our fight is first spiritual and most of that fight goes on between our ears.

God has given us weapons to fight with and they are "mighty in God". Powerless in and of themselves, but in God they are mighty, powerful and able to bring those thoughts under control. They break down the mightiest stronghold. These weapons include the Word of God (Ephesians 6:17), prayer (Ephesians 6:18) and the anointing of the Holy Spirit (Acts 1:8).

One of the ways you use the Word of God as a weapon is to personalize it for you. It is no good as black ink on a white page but actually in your hand, it's a sword that kicks mental butt!

Declare What the Word Says About You While God Works on Your Problem

Personalize Jeremiah 29:11 by saying, «I know that God has plans to prosper me. I know that God has a hope and a future for me and I know those plans are good and I know that they will come to pass because God said they would.»

Let it be said of you, the reason why those behind you live in victory is because you chose to oppose and defeat an oppressive enemy in the battle between your ears.

NOTES AND QUOTES

_____

_____

_____

_____

_____

_____

_____

_____

_____

"Love does not begin and end the way we seem to think it does. Love is a battle, love is a war; love is a growing up." James A. Baldwin: American novelist, essayist, playwright, poet, and social critic.

"I firmly believe that any man's finest hour, the greatest fulfillment of all that he holds dear, is that moment when he has worked his heart out in a good cause and lies exhausted on the field of battle - victorious." Vince Lombardi : Legendary American Football Coach

HISTORICALLY SPEAKING, PAYBACK DOESN'T WORK

If you ever had reason to drive west of Utley, Texas, it would be easy to pass up the historical marker on the south side of FM 969. But if you did have time to stop and see what it says, it would tell you very little about what actually happened there. It's a place where people lived and died 171 years ago. A place where both dreams and nightmares came true.

FRONTIER FAMILY

One of the brave families who settled the frontier lived here when it was a lot easier to die than to actually live. Texas had just won her independence from Mexico, and the Coleman family settled on land deeded to them by Austin himself.

Robert and Elizabeth Coleman fought the Mexicans, the Comanches and the harsh Texas elements while scratching the ground for food and having babies. They lived with very little comfort on the Colorado River, and Robert commanded the fort nearby. They looked forward to a day where living would be less dangerous and survival more likely, but Robert never saw that day.

In 1837, Robert drowned in the Brazos River, and Elizabeth did not have the luxury to spend a season in mourning. Now she was a single mother with a three year old boy, a twelve year old boy and several daughters whose ages are not known to us now. For the next two years, she successfully fought and lived harder than most can imagine, nearly completely isolated from the rest of the world.

By then, her oldest boy Albert was fourteen, and he was a huge help in every way. The Coleman daughters had never known anything but frontier life, and they fit well into the rhythm of the farm. Tommy was now five and spent his days chasing rabbits and catching horned toads.

INDIAN BLOODBATH

On February 18, 1839, Elizabeth was working in the garden when she saw a raiding party of Comanche Indians coming full gallop towards the house. She screamed to the kids to get inside and for Albert to prepare to defend himself. Little Tommy was too far away to make it to the house in time, and as Elizabeth stood in the doorway, an Indian arrow pierced her throat. She fell where she stood in a bloody clump of writhing panic. As Albert frantically dragged her past the threshold, a Comanche picked up Tommy for parts unknown.

Albert fired off a shot from his muzzleloader while his mother lay gurgling, and his sisters continued screaming from under the bed.

In the chaos and panic, I would imagine Albert found it difficult to reload the awkward rifle. He had no idea a Comanche warrior had his sights on him through a crack in the side of the house.

AFTERMATH

Several hours later, would-be rescuers arrived to find Tommy had been kidnapped and Albert, Elizabeth and one Comanche warrior dead. The girls were still under the bed and had to be pried away from their hiding place: a fairly common scene in early Texas history. An injustice barely comprehensible. The settlers vowed revenge for the horrific act of savagery, and they would have it.

THE REST OF THE STORY

If after reading this, your blood is boiling a little, as it should, let me tell you another part of this same story. Like you, Elizabeth had no way of knowing, not that she would have cared, that the Comanches assaulting her were the surviving remnant of an Indian village who had just been massacred by settlers.

Four days earlier on February 14th, John Henry Moore had taken a Texan raiding party to find Indians and attacked a village at sunrise on the San Saba River. Besides warriors, women, children and the elderly were cut down, indiscriminately shot and left for dead. The surviving Comanches vowed revenge for the horrific act of savagery, and they would have it in the Coleman family, miles away.

Now before your blood boils at John Moore, as it should, let me tell you another part of this story. John Henry Moore was hunting Indians in retaliation of an attack on another family, and those Indians were hunting settlers in retaliation of another attack on an Indian village. The Cycle of Death goes on and on until the biggest group with the biggest gun wins, and that's what happened. These stories are tragic and horrific.

IT A'INT YOURS

Revenge does not belong to us. It belongs to God. Mama taught me a long time ago not to take what doesn't belong to me, and the Brewer is reminding you to do the same. Revenge in the hands of a Holy God is a Holy thing. Revenge in the hands of somebody like me is an ugly thing that does more damage and very little good. Revenge in God's hand brings Justice, but in our hands brings evil, even on innocent people. Next time you and I have trouble believing that, we should think about poor Albert trying to drag his mama in the house with an arrow through her throat or the panic and terror that little Indian girl must have felt as she took her last breath on the San Saba.

Forgiveness and trusting in the Lord to make things right comes from God Himself. Revenge belongs to Him. The choice to not be a bigger part of the problem belongs to you and me.

NOTES AND QUOTES

_____
_____
_____
_____
_____
_____
_____
_____
_____
_____
_____
_____
_____
_____
_____
_____

Deuteronomy 32:35
Vengeance is Mine, and recompense...

"Always forgive your Enemies, Nothing annoys them so much."
-Oscar Wilde

"The best revenge is massive success." - Frank Sinatra

"Gorgeous hair the nest revenge." - Ivana Trump

"There is no revenge so complete as forgiveness." -Josh Billings

A WORD ON CADDO FRIENDSHIP

Four hundred years ago the valleys and tributaries of the Ouachita, Red, Sabine, and Neches Rivers in what is today known as the Ark-La-Tex region were home to an extraordinary society of people. They were farmers, warriors, potters, and traders with a unique culture, the ancestors of the people known today as the Caddo Indians.

The Brewer lives in the shadow of a hill in Johnson County known as Caddo Peak. When I was a kid you could drive up there and I found my very first arrow head on what used to be an important site to the Caddo who had been relocated here in the 1800's.

Before my town Joshua was named after the Biblical hero that took the promised land, our community was actually known as Caddo Grove and was a stone's throw away from my house on what would be the Chisholm Trail and much later farm and market road 1902.

NATIVE TEXAN

At one time the Caddo were a powerful and heavily populated people, who formed a society that early Spanish explorers highly regarded as civilized and friendly in comparison to other neighbors. Sadly, this initial respect did not spare the Caddo from the common fate of so many of the native folk who came into contact with European diseases, guns, and agendas. In less than two hundred years, the mighty Caddo were reduced to a few hundred refugees who were uprooted again from Johnson county and assigned tiny parcels of land in the Oklahoma Indian Territories before being up rooted yet again in the Oklahoma land grab.

Like the ancient Jews before them, against all odds, the Caddo survived the 1800s and today, according to the Caddo Nation of Oklahoma, number more than 4000. An interesting thing about the Caddo is that they don't live on a reservation and most of them don't even live in Oklahoma. They live in houses and apartments all throughout America working as police officers, nurses, lawyers, electricians, artists and the whole gamut. It seems that the Caddo have always been the friend of America even though America has not always been the friend of the Caddo.

Tejas is the Spanish spelling of a Caddo word taysha, which means "friend" or "ally." In the 17th century the Spanish knew the western most Caddo people as "The great kingdom of Tejas" and the name lived on to become the name of the 28th state of the United States and the coolest place on the planet -Texas. The tradition continued all the way through and became the official motto of the state of Texas -Friendship.

How ironic that the name Texas comes from the word meaning friendship from a people that Texas would not be the friend of. Sometimes you are the friend of somebody that isn't really your friend at all.

INDIAN GIVER

Not only am I the key pounding coffee drinker that churns up newspaper columns, but I am also the Senior Pastor of Open Door Ministries in Joshua, TX. One of the things I have a hard time convincing people is that Jesus Christ is your friend; He's the kind of friend to us that the Caddo Indians have been to Texas.

What I mean to say - is that Jesus has been feared because He's different than us, blamed for things he didn't do, hated because

His presence doesn't go along with our life styles and ultimately kicked out of our lives, yet He is famous for friendship. He didn't just die for you. He died and went to hell for you, slapping death in the face because you and I couldn't. He has proven Himself to be the kind of friend that only He can be. Let's not do to him what we as Texans have done to our friends the Caddo Indians. Let's keep Jesus close and not throw him out of our lives.

"Greater love hath no man than this, that a man lay down his life for his friends." (John 15:13)

NOTES AND QUOTES _____

_____
_____
_____
_____
_____
_____
_____
_____

"But I want to play with Walter, Aunty, why can't I?" She took off her glasses and stared at me. "I'll tell you why," she said, "Because- he – is – trash, that's why you can't play with him" - HARPER LEE. From To Kill a Mockingbird

"Racism isn't born folks. It's taught. I have a 2 year old son and you know what he hates? Naps! That's it! End of list." -Denis Leary : American Comedian, Actor.

"Racism is the refuge of freaked out and ignorant people." -Troy Brewer : famous for quoting all 50 states in alphabetical order in less than 25 seconds.

The Brewer with a bunch of his hillbilly Ugandans 2014

FREEDOM FIGHTER

THAT'S 70'S SHOW

7th grade at Joshua middle school was a great year for me. Back in 1979 it was principled by the very man it's named after now. Mr. Loflin ran the school, Coach Nichols ruled the roost, but a man named Dub Crocker taught the Texas history class.

It was a very political class for seventh graders because Mr. Crocker, was all fired up about the mess America was in at the time. Before I finished 7th grade I understood what an interest rate was and I knew that it was at 24% for house mortgages and that I should be outraged over that. That same year, I learned where Panama was and I knew that President Carter had given it away and that I should have been upset. "Teddy Roosevelt was rolling in his grave," I learned.

Though I had never heard of Iran before the 7th grade I knew that we had hostages there and our American embassy was taken over because everybody knew we were a bunch of "Pushovers" that wouldn't do anything.

What did that have to with Texas History? Well, Mr. Crocker saw the world in terms of how it affected Texas. He was a Texan and that's the way most of us Texans see things.

GONE TO TEXAS

Out of all the things I learned in that incredible year, there is one thing that he introduced me to that started a life-long fascination and passion that continues today. I had heard about the Alamo before 7th grade but not like he taught it. We actually studied the 13 day siege and the three warriors that some would revere as the trinity itself. Travis, Bowie and the coon- skinned cap wearing "Lion of the West", Davey Crocket.

You don't have to be black to revere Martin Luther King Jr as an amazingly great man and you don't have to be Catholic to love Mother Theresa as an awesome woman. Just like that, you don't have to be Texan to love Travis and the guys at the Alamo.

FREEDOM FIGHTER

I have read more than a dozen books on the subject and actually visited the shrine of Texas at least thirty times.

In my tripped out mind, Crocket is still on those adobe walls firing against all odds and Houston is still on his white horse in full gallop towards Santa Anna's tent. Call me a sap but I love the romantic notion of freedom fighting.

On March 3, 1836 William Barret Travis frantically scribbled a few lines while under cannon siege.

"Take care of my little boy. If the country should be saved, I may make for him a splendid fortune; but if the country be lost and I should perish, he will have nothing but the proud recollection that he is the son of a man who died for his country."

Travis loved freedom and the letter to David Ayers is the last known letter written by Travis before the fall of the Alamo on the morning of March 6. Travis died at his post in hand to hand combat on the cannon platform at the northeast corner of the fortress. He was 26 years old.

Houston, Travis, Austin, Crocket, Seguin, Bowie and Bonham set a standard for all of Texas that followed them. A tradition and heritage of Freedom, guts and rugged individualism.

GOD AND TEXAS

It is the nature of people to conform to the image of what makes them tick. It is a biblical principle and a matter of fact that God made us to take on the characteristics of the things we love. Whether it's heavy metal, the military or Nascar, if you look at something long enough-you start to look like it.

Because of this principle, I have noticed that while not all revolutionaries are Godly people, all Godly people are revolutionaries in one way or another. A true characteristic of the love of God is to hate bondage and oppression.

Nearly 2000 years before Travis fell at the Alamo, Jesus Christ was lifted on the cross.

He hated the oppression and bondage of sin so much that he was willing to die to overcome it. He loved humanity and wanted us to be set free so bad that he was willing to give his own life on our behalf. He didn't die for nothing, he died and rose again so that you and I could have a real shot at true freedom.

Jesus is not your warden, He is your deliverer and as the bible says, he whom the Son sets free is free in deed. In Galatians 5:1 Paul declares "It is for Freedom Christ has set us free. God loves to scrap for your freedom friend, so take advantage of it. It is the Brewer's humble opinion that only through Christ will you find the freedom to forgive, to have joy, to have peace, to love God and to pursue a life of passion that really makes a difference. Freedom isn't for wimps but it's offered to everybody.

The Lord Himself is warrior who thought so much of you He was willing to fight and die for you. His fight for your freedom continues and he's counting on you to win the battle. He has already won the war.

NOTES AND QUOTES

_____

_____

_____

_____

_____

_____

_____

_____

_____

_____

_____

_____

_____

_____

_____

_____

_____

_____

_____

_____

_____

_____

"Caged birds accept each other but flight is what they long for."
– Tennessee Williams

"Expose yourself to your deepest fear; after that, fear has no power, and the fear of freedom shrinks and vanishes. You are free." - Jim Morrison

"God wants us to take on hell with a water pistol and scream at every kind of bondage there is. We are supposed to be freedom fanatics." -Troy Brewer

THE WAY OF THE WARIOR

This last week was my Dad's 66th birthday. Being the magnificent answered prayer of a son that I am, I took dad off for three days of R and R and a whirlwind tour of Texas colonial battlefields. It was a hoot.

I get my love of History and all things Texas from my Dad. He totally buys into the mythical side of our glorious history. So there we were, out stomping around on places preserved and some barely marked because we are nerds and proud of it.

Our smorgasbord of Texas warfare included these items on the Menu.

The old Coleman House.
Elizabeth Coleman looked up from her garden just in time to see 300 Comanche warriors attacking her farm in 1847. It turned out to be a really bad day for her and her kids. We drove past the place some thirty miles East of Austin.

The battle site of Brushy Creek.
In the heat of battle against the Comanches who murdered Elizabeth Coleman, Killed young Albert Coleman and kidnapped her 5 year old, a man named Burleson knew he could not win with just one man and a 14 year old boy. There at Brushy Creek, Burleson shouted to the pair to get back on their horses and retreat. Just as Burleson started to spur his horse into a run for safety, he saw that the teenager was having trouble getting back onto his nervous mount. Burleson jumped out of his saddle to lend a hand and caught an Indian bullet in the back of his head.

He dropped dead as the boy climbed onto the horse and escaped with his life. His older brother, Edward Burleson, a brigadier general in the militia, soon arrived with reinforcements. There at Brushy Creek, the general rode after the Indians who had killed his brother.

Dad and I went out there just to feel the dirt and smell the air, again, because we are nerds.

We also went to the Alamo, Washington on the Brazos and even San Fillip.

All told, we covered about 500 miles on our journey of Texas Battle fields. Being somewhat of a wordsmith I entitled our trip, "The way of the warrior."

A WARRIOR BRIDE

Part of my love for battlefields doesn't just come from my six generations as a Texan. It comes from the Kingdom of God. Jesus is a king but know for certain that He is a Warrior King.

Revelation 21:8 informs us that there are no wimps or cowards in Heaven. That makes heaven all the more glorious to me. We are called the bride of Christ which means we are totally fixated on the bride groom, but know this, we are a warrior bride. Undefeated and fully capable. Confident, positive and at full ease in an environment that is otherwise hostile.

There is more victory attached to you than you can even imagine. Here are just a few of the Brewer's notes on the walk of Christians which is every bit the way of a warrior.

We are not Spectators, we are Warriors!
One of the world famous "decisions that define us" from the same titled book by Dave Crone is "We have decided to be the ones telling the stories of God's power - not the ones hearing about them." That is a decision all of us need to make.

There should be no separation between the pew and the pulpit or the sacred and secular. All of the church belongs to Jesus so get up, get out and get after it! An adventure in Life is waiting for you.

COMFORT KILLS!

Jesus says in Luke 10:3 that he is sending us out as lambs among wolves, not a potatoes among couches. We are not tourists on vacation and life is not a perpetual spa experience. Our God given ability to hang in there when things are extremely tough is essential to the way of a warrior and paramount for victory. Remember, "Better" is better but better will not be easier or more comfortable.

We are called to be peace makers not peace keepers. I like to think of the ill relevance of so called peace keeping forces throughout the world as they stand by and watch a million massacred in places like Rwanda. I also remember the effectiveness of the Texas Rangers with a pistol called a peace maker. The way of the warrior is all about peace making not in making deals with the enemy.

We do not have to be defeated by a defeated devil! My friend, Graham Cooke says this in his book series, *The Way of the Warrior*.

"We can weary him with our rest. We can discourage him by our faith. We can demoralize him by our joy. We can depress him by our endurance. We can dispirit him by our favor..." *Qualities of a Spiritual Warrior (The Way of the Warrior) Book 1 by Graham Cooke*

BRILLIANT BOOK HOUSE

I agree with you Graham.

The way of the warrior is attached to the passionate heart of the King of Kings himself. I want to encourage you as you read this, to know that there is still a lot of living for you to do. Jesus is not just the strength giver but actually is your strength all together. So, now that you know you were born to be a bad motor scooter, I think it is high time you and I become who we really have been all along and just didn't know it.

Romans 8:19 (NIV)
The creation waits in eager expectation for the sons of God to be revealed.

NOTES AND QUOTES

_____
_____
_____
_____
_____
_____
_____
_____
_____
_____

"Rest in this-it is His business to lead, command,
impel, send, call, or whatever you want to call it.
It is your business to obey, follow, move, respond,
or what have you... The sound of 'gentle stillness'
after all the thunder and wind have passed
will be the ultimate Word from God."
-Jim Elliot

BIG BEND NATIONAL PARK 2012

SPARTANS, TEXANS AND WARRIOR KINGS

Almost 500 years before Christ, a Spartan army of only 300 men stood against a million or so Persians at a place called Thermopylae. Now the Brewer is not particularly a big fan of ancient Spartans. Besides destroying the fair city my mama named me after with a stinking wooden horse, they were also known to be racist and Pagans that had no mercy for anyone. With that said, the Texan in me can't help but love the astonishing quality of warriors they produced.

The King that is so famous for this military miracle was a guy by the name of Leonidas. What I just love about King Leonidas is that he wasn't just a king, he was a warrior King. He didn't sit on a golden throne and order men to fight. He fought out front of all his men and invited them to fight with him. I love the whole idea of a warrior king.

Almost two hundred years later another warrior king rose from the same part of the world but this one would be remembered as "Great". Alexander conquered the known world not for any righteous reason but just because he wanted to. Before it was over, millions would be dead and many more hurting because of Alexander's ambition of conquest. Though I don't much care for his empire any better, I can't help but love the fact that he was a warrior King.

After Alexander turned south on the Indus River he encountered a warlike clan called the Mali. After building siege weapons and ladders they attacked the walled city and Alexander was the first one over the walls. He was so far ahead of the rest of his men that he actually engaged the entire army by his self while his men scrambled to keep up with him. With an arrow in his lung and a sword in his hand Alexander the great fought in hand-to-hand combat until his men were able to subdue the enemy. I love a warrior King.

Almost 2300 years later on holy ground that would be called Texas, a General with a righteous cause, raced across the San Jacinto battlefield. Though vastly outnumbered and in broad day light, Sam Houston was so far ahead of the rest of his men that he drew all the fire of the Mexican dictator's troops. Having two horses shot out from under him, he limped towards the enemy with pointed sword yelling, "Remember the Alamo, Remember Goliad!"

Sam Houston would soon be the President of the nation of Texas. Though he was a political leader he was also a proven warrior. I love a warrior King.

Being a fairly famous Jesus freak with ever growing popularity, I get a lot of letters and e-mails. Most of them cuss me out but there are more asking me what denomination or nondenominational group I subscribe to. I am for whatever in Christianity is wimp free. Sign me up with the Christians that have the guts to be Christians in a day where men act more like women than men. Show me those Christians that are not just talking about the love of God but actually demonstrating it through the hard work it takes to make a real difference in somebody's life. Put me in line with the people that are living proof that God never consults your history before giving you a future.

You see; real Christians don't just serve a King. They serve a passionate, warrior King and those of us that follow him live a lifetime of learning how to get out of His way and let him fight like He wants to. Not only is Christ not scared of the battles that you and I face, he actually gets excited about the prospect of another glorious scrap. That's the way our King is. Unlike any we have ever seen before, He's compassionate, ready to serve, approachable and full of mercy but make no mistake about it. He is a warrior King.

Exodus 15:3
The LORD is a man of war: the LORD is his name.

NOTES AND QUOTES

_____
_____
_____
_____
_____
_____
_____
_____
_____
_____
_____
_____
_____
_____
_____
_____
_____
_____
_____
_____
_____
_____
_____

"For those who fight for it,
life has a flavor the protected never know."
Sign at Khe Sanh, Vietnam 1968

A TALE OF TWO ENEMIES

It was December 7, 1941. The time was 7:49 on an early Sunday morning. Commander Mitsuo Fuchida was leading a squadron of 360 Japanese fighters that would prophetically turn the whole war full circle that day.

Seeing the fleet peacefully at anchor 9,000 feet below his plane, Fuchida dove out of a white cloud then radioed back to the Japanese fleet saying, "Tora, tora, tora!" The attack on Pearl Harbor had begun.

The smoking carnage of the surprise attack left an aftermath of five destroyed battleships and fourteen others sunk or damaged. It was a great day for Fuchida and the last day for more than 2,300 Americans. A day, one might say, of infamy.

On the other side of the Pacific, a sergeant by the name of Jacob DeShazer was peeling potatoes at his base in Oregon. Not long after, DeShazer would have the opportunity to volunteer for a special squadron lead by Colonel Jimmy Doolittle. This top-secret mission would dare to directly bomb Tokyo and the heart of the hated Japanese. Jacob couldn't sign up fast enough.

By all accounts, Doolittle's raid was a stunning success, but DeShazer's B-24 bomber ran out of fuel before it reached a safe place in China. Forced to bail out over Japanese-held territory, DeShazer was captured and spent the next 40 months of his life as a prisoner of war. He spent 34 of those months in solitary confinement and was routinely tortured by his captors. As he watched fellow American prisoners horribly tortured and executed or starved to death, DeShazer remained alive— and so did his hatred for the Japanese.

Fuchida, on the other hand, was celebrated as the undisputed Japanese "Hero of Pearl Harbor." In 1942, he came down with a case of appendicitis and was unable to fly. That attack probably saved his life because he missed the battle of Midway where the Japanese Navy was soundly defeated.

A few years later, Fuchida narrowly missed death again when he was ordered to leave Hiroshima the very day before the nuclear bomb was dropped. The hated Americans were killing everyone he knew, it seemed. Just as Fuchida barely escaped death throughout the war, so did Deshazer in the Japanese prison camp.

Solitary confinement gave DeShazer time to chew on the subject of hatred. Clinging to life, he yearned to know God and begged his guards for a Bible.

Two years later, he finally received one and poured through the pages. When thumbing through the text, his eyes fell on the passage where Jesus cried out from the cross, "Father, forgive them. They know not what they do." The black ink on the white page became words in his heart that would change him forever.

He later wrote, "I discovered that when I looked at the enemy officers and guards who had starved and beaten my companions and me so cruelly, I found my bitter hatred for them changed to loving pity . . . . I prayed for God to forgive my torturers, and I determined by the aid of Christ, to do my best to acquaint these people with the message of salvation."

On Aug. 20, 1945, a smiling Japanese guard swung open DeShazer's cell door and said, "War over. You go home now." A few days later Americans parachuted into the camp and sent the prisoners to hospitals where they would slowly recover.

Jacob finally got to go to his beloved home, but he didn't stay there long. His Christian transformation was so dramatic he went back to Japan, but this time as a missionary. No longer hating the Japanese, he wanted to make a difference there.

Fast forward now to one day in October 1948. While getting off the train in Tokyo, Fuchida, the Japanese war hero, now a farmer, saw an American handing out leaflets in Japanese. The title caught his eye: I Was a Prisoner of Japan. It grabbed his attention, especially the part about Pearl Harbor. Even though they had been enemies, Fuchida had admired the courage of the Doolittle Raiders. He continued reading.

The whole Christianity thing was a big surprise to Fuchida. A friend told him to get a Bible, but Fuchida could not find one in Japanese. Just a few days later, on the same train platform, a Japanese man stood with boxes of books. "Get your Bible. It is food for your soul," the man cried in Japanese. Struck by the coincidence, and despite his Shinto heritage, he bought one.

The opened Bible fell to Luke 23:34, and he read those words for the very first time, "Father, forgive them, for they know not what they do."

Fuchida later wrote, "I was impressed that I was certainly one of those for whom Jesus had prayed. The many men I had killed had been slaughtered in the name of patriotism, for I did not understand the love of Christ."

He changed from a bitter ex-war hero to a man on a new mission. Fuchida went on to become an evangelist throughout Japan and Asia. He and DeShazer eventually became very close friends.

The Brewer salutes them both as we think about the cross at this Easter time.

Good Friday was only good because of the one being executed and the goodness of God still leads men to repentance today.

*The Brewer Chummin' up to an African Witch Doctor
in Sierra Leone. 2011*

CHAPTER THREE
THEOLOGY AND THE EVER MOVING DOCTRINE OF BREWER

I think it is normal, in any relationship, for the joy of discovery to be ongoing. I know that this is especially true for my relationship with Jesus.

There are things I believe now that I didn't a few years ago and things I used to make a big deal out of that are way on my back burner in my walk with Christ now. Again, this is normal.

There is not very much normal or I should say, really traditional about what I am believing God for these days and this section contains some of my rants on what I believe.

Everybody has a little different spin on how they see and hear God. For me, my spin is all over the map but basic. It's got to be real, it's got to be powerful and it's got to be about Jesus being awesome.

The Brewer preaching at a church in Kingsville, Texas. 2013

CLASSIC CHRISTIANITY

Revisiting a classic is always a little risky. I've lost count of the number of films that I was convinced would never date which seem kind of cheesy now. Not that the twist in the movie was cheesy, but the general coolness of the entire scenario. There are those that I enjoy just as much today as I did back then while hearing smaller minds scoff at them.

There are some classics that in the midst of tipping a few tacky meters -just have to be revisited and appreciated. How can you not love the jaw dropping wonder of a classic twist or ending? As a writer I do my best to avoid exclamation marks but there's no way to properly express the following spoilers without animated written expletive.

Charlton Heston finds the Statue of Liberty and realizes he's been on the earth the whole time.

What?! Soylent Green is made out of people? You gotta be kidding me!!

Darth Vader is Luke Skywalker's dad! How's that work?

Bruce Willis has been dead through the whole film and he doesn't know it! Good-googly-moogly!!!

THE RETURN OF THE CLASSIC.

In 1985, Coke was starting to lose the cola war to Pepsi so they ditched the original for something a little more marketable. The outcry that followed was so incredible they halted production the same week they released it on the public. Twenty-three years later we can see a revival of classic things from movie remakes to the return of the American muscle car. Most of us love classic things.

The Brewer subscribes to Classic Christianity. You know the kind that says it's not about your history but all about your destiny. A return of Spirit-breathed living that is focused around a real life, resurrected, everything changer. The hope for Heaven yes but the pursuit of abundant life like only the guy who has slapped death in the face can offer.

I think the original Classic Christianity is totally fixated on the intimate personal on-going encounter with the King of the Universe and the result is a never ending transformation into better and better and better. Oh how the Brewer loves to gulp on that! There's another one of those exclamation marks I am not supposed to be printing.

Anyway, Classic Christianity says I have a problem and Christ is the solution. Classic Christianity also says through Him, I cease to be the problem and play a vital role in carrying out the solution. There are just so many things I love about this incredible journey of living life naturally supernatural.

Sadly, a lot of people think a return to classic Christianity would be a return to past methods and techniques. There are those among us that really believe living a Godly Christian life means to lock in on a lifestyle of a certain era of time. This kind of accepted wisdom spills over into the ideas of dress, language and the official size and conduct of a church service. The Brewer humbly submits such thinking, while well intentioned towards an attempt at holiness, comes from a demonic spirit called stupid. Something we have always struggled with.

It is the nature of an unredeemed mind to always be looking back. Jesus mentioned this when he spoke on 'Lot's wife' and even He didn't know her by name -that's probably not good. I am not saying we should lock arms with the world, I am just saying that we should be free to go farther and dream a different dream than others before us.

Dave Crone from the Mission in Vacaville California says the Pharisees were the dream killers of Jesus's day and he's exactly right. If you see somebody today, thumping a Bible the same way we did a long time ago and doing everything within his power to put you in a religious box, know that he is the same kind of person who nailed Jesus to a board and hung him up naked. For your sake, run from him, for our sake run him over.

While I believe without apology that the church of Jesus Christ is the only boat afloat, I also believe a lot of us on board don't understand the heart of the Captain. The Kingdom is progressive. Who knew? His kingdom is without end. There are no limitations and there is no place in the fullness of the world that doesn't belong to him. Go figure.

As long as people make methods and the function of the church as the priority of Christianity instead of relationship to God first and to other people 2nd, the greatest threat to a new move of God will always be the last one.

God help us and save us from the futile attempt of doing Christianity. Propel us instead to live the adventure and responsibility of actually being Christians.

NOTES and QUOTES _____

_____
_____
_____

"Christians are hard to tolerate; I don't know how Jesus does it"
– Bono: Singer, Writer, Activist, Rockstar

ALL THE RIGHT REASONS TO ASK
THE WRONG QUESTIONS

30 years ago, my 6th grade teacher at Joshua Middle School stood me up and told me that there was no such thing as a stupid question. Instead of being encouraged as she thought I would, I was challenged to try and come up with as many obviously stupid questions I could conjure. It set me on a lifetime of loving to propose ridiculous queries just for the sake of entertainment. I would like to publicly apologize for tormenting that poor woman and actually thank her for years of mindless entertainment. Here are a few of those I am talking about.

STUPID QUESTIONS

I would like to ask people who are for the ethical treatment of animals, is it ok for Vegetarians to eat animal crackers? My good friend Tommy Cole down at the Mountain Valley Funeral Home might be able to answer this one. If a funeral procession was at night, do you think we would drive with our headlights off?

IT GETS WORSE

If a turtle doesn't have a shell, would he be called homeless or naked? When sign makers go on strike, is anything written on their signs? Would you call a fly without wings a walk?

MUCH WORSE

Did Adam and Eve have belly buttons? Why isn't there mouse flavored cat food? If you only have one eye can you still get double vision?

BRILLIANT ANSWERS

Because of my love for stupid questions I have become a fount of otherwise useless information. Life is too short to not know that the K in K-mart comes from the company's founder, Sebastian Spering Kresge, who opened his first store in 1899.

I could not bear to wake up in the morning without knowing that C.W. Post came up with the name "Grape Nuts" because the cereal contained maltose, which he thought was "grape sugar" and because the crunch reminded him of nuts.

WHY ASK WHY?

This crazy world we live in produces so many curveballs and blind-sided ninja slaps that it becomes easy for us to sit ourselves in a place where we need to know answers. When it comes to life's big questions, if we are not careful we will find ourselves stuck on a question we can't get past. Like a needle on an old record player we repeat, "Why, why, why, why, why?"

As a Christian I find myself connected to the pain and the grief of those around me and as a Texan I find myself in unwanted territory more times than I can count. In those tough places we will never find the right answers if we insist on asking the wrong questions.

We can never expect a right answer when we demand to know why from our creator. Why is the wrong question and though we may feel like we have the right to ask the whys of life, the Christian world view is that it is in fact an invalid question. Sticking with invalid questions will make us invalid or paralyzed, unable to move forward and to progress.

As God pointed out to biblical Job, we are not qualified to ask the whys of life. Until we can wrap our heads around the mysteries of this universe we simply are not capable or even eligible for the why answers. So until then it just isn't productive to demand a question when there is no way you can swallow the answer.

THE RIGHT QUESTIONS

In Acts chapter 2 we have the true account of the supernatural power of God's Holy Spirit descending on believers at the day of Pentecost. There within the text are at least two of the right questions we should be asking. The first one is "What does this mean?" and the 2nd is "What should I do?"

When you ask why, it is connected to your pain and your grief and your personal hurt. "What does this mean?" is a question for "Big Picture" thinkers and it is attached to God's purpose. "What should I do?" is attached to humility and adds legs to your faith. These are valid questions for people looking for the true answers that God is willing to answer.

For this short life span, we don't get most of the whys of life answered. That's for later when we "know as we are known." Until then, we are offered the person of Christ Himself as the very answer to all of life's riddles and that's an offer none of us should refuse.

There is nothing wrong with asking questions as long as we do not use questions to oppose God in our thinking.

Romans 14:19
Let us therefore follow after the things which make for peace

NOTES: _____
_____
_____
_____

"It's not God who's messed up, it's the screamers who say they believe in him and who claim to pursue their ends in his holy name." – John Irving : American novelist and Academy Award-winning screenwriter

A little chat before her baptism.

HOMECOMING HEROES AND
APPRECIATED ACCOLADES

A HEROES WELCOME

On any given day of the week, more than 100 soldiers come through DFW Airport on their way home for two weeks of long awaited R & R. Under that program, American soldiers receive these little vacations from stressful and risky war tours in Iraq and Afghanistan.

Thirty-five years ago most veterans came home from the nightmare of Vietnam, only to be spit on by a Jane Fonda fan. Most passed through crowds of people that wouldn't even look them in the eye, much less acknowledge their selfless service.

This aint the seventies and this aint the people's republic of Berkley. The Brewer tips his glorious hat to DFW Airport for hosting a program called "Welcome Home a Hero". It's a thoughtful and selfless outreach where volunteers celebrate these men and women as they come through the customs door. They give them hugs, pats on the back, throw babies in the air and take lots of pictures.

They tell these jaw dropped soldiers that they are proud of them and that they appreciate them. The impact it makes is a life-long one not just for the military but also for their kids and family looking on.

You don't have to agree with the war against terrorism to agree it is incredible folks who will go out of their way to encourage someone during a perilous time in their life. Homecomings are so important.

GOING HOME

Some of my favorite memories are from seeing my family after a long trip overseas. Last July I spent the month in India and when I finally made it back to DFW my bride, four kids and lots of friends from my church were there at midnight to tell me they loved me. I tried so hard not to bawl and squall. It was a great day to be alive.

When I think of homecomings though, I just can't help but think about Heaven. I have had the privilege of preaching some funerals for very close friends and to me they were something like a home going. I don't think Heaven is the place you go to after you leave home. I think heaven is the home you go to after you leave this place.

My good friend and personal secretary Paula Ledbetter went home having to leave her husband John and three boys here in Johnson County. As tragic of a loss as it was for those of us that knew Paula, there was no doubt that Paula had graduated with honors and gone home to her reward. Over 600 people crammed into a tiny place to celebrate her 37 years and at least 17 were so inspired by her life; they became Christians themselves that weekend.

When you get home from a long hard day, the bad things don't really matter because your home after all. I think heaven is like that.

ALMOST THERE

About 100 years ago there was a missionary by the name of Samuel Morrison. Samuel spent the last 25 years of his life as a medical missionary in the darkest regions of Africa. When he came down with a terminal illness, he decided to go back to the United States to die and it just so happened he traveled on the same ocean liner that brought President Teddy Roosevelt back from his famous hunting expedition.

When that great ship pulled into New York harbor it looked like the entire population of America showed up to greet the president. Bands were playing, banners were waving, choirs were singing, balloons were flying, flashbulbs were popping, and newsreels were poised to record the return of the president. Mr. Roosevelt stepped down the gangplank to thunderous cheers and applause.

Now at the same time this was going on, frail Samuel Morrison exhausted and worn out, limped off the boat at the other end. No one was there to greet him. He slowly made his way through the mob. There were so many people there he couldn't even find a cab.

Inside his broken heart he began to sadly complain, "Lord the president has been in Africa for 3 weeks killing animals and the whole world turns out to welcome him home. I've been in Africa for 25 years serving you and not one person has greeted me or even knows I'm here." No sooner had he said those things when in the quietness of his heart, a gentle loving voice whispered, "My child, you're not yet home."

———————————

"Behold, I am coming soon! My reward is with me, and I will give to everyone according to what he has done. I am the Alpha and the Omega, the First and the Last, the Beginning and the End." Revelation 22:12-13

NOTES and QUOTES

_____
_____
_____
_____

"When I stand before God at the end of my life, I would hope that I would not have a single bit of talent left, and could say, 'I used everything you gave me." – Erma Bombeck : American humorist and writter

Jerusalem 2013

ENTER THE DRAGON

The year was 1975 and the Brewer was a nine year old with a heavy Texas accent and a mind full of mush. My folks took me to the Seminary South movie theater in Ft. Worth to see a film that would have a profound effect on our culture, our generation and yes, even me.

JAWS is not a movie about deep human insight and it doesn't have any kind of profound philosophical message, yet there probably is not another film that made a bigger impact on any one society.

Thirty-two years later, the impact is just as effective as it was back then. It doesn't matter if you are in fresh or salt water, that famous John Williams sound track starts to play in your head. We no longer feel safe in the water.

TOOTHLESS

While the fear may be very real, the threat is really not. There are over 10,000 miles of American coastline. Millions of people swim in those waters and every year there are fewer than twelve shark attacks. Most of those are provoked and usually only one or two are fatal. None of that matters though when you are the guy in the water and the JAWS music is bouncing between your ears.

The odds of you being eaten by a shark in American water are astronomical. I tell myself this every time I swim in the ocean; because I'm convinced I'm going to hit the shark lotto.

LIGHT EM IF YOU'VE GOT EM

While all of us worry about sharks, we very seldom worry about things like lightning strikes. I think the threat is very real when it comes to lightning. In 1985 alone there were 600 people killed in America by lightning and over the past 100 years there have been over 24,000 people lit up and sent to eternity with a thunderclap. Those are just the people we know of.

Attacks by grizzly bears are relatively rare and sporadic. Yet I'm scared of a big ol' bear getting me when I'm in a national park. A total of 162 bear-inflicted injuries were reported from 1900 through 1985 in Canadian and American national parks. The truth is there were only 19 human deaths from grizzly attacks documented in the national parks in North America and an additional 22 deaths in Alaska outside the parks.

In my mind, there must have been thousands killed by grizzlies over the past century but it's just not true. In the history of the United States there have only been 20 reports of death by black bears and only 13 by mountain lions.

For each person killed by a mountain lion in the past 100 years, 300 people have died from bee stings. I'm not scared of bees, but when I'm in Big Bend National Park I am thinking about mountain lions. Yet the truth is that for each person killed by a mountain lion in the past 100 years, 750 people have died when their cars collided with a deer.

That's not something I fret over. For each person killed by a mountain lion in the past 100 years, 1,100 people have been killed in hunting accidents.

I could go on and on but the bottom line is that a lot of our fears are really not warranted at all. In fact a lot of the mental battles we fight are over things that are not even existent. We tend to exhaust ourselves on fantasized battlefields of endless "what if" rabbit trails.

DRAGON SLAYER

So much of the strife in our very limited brain space is over things that are not even actually going on.

I call these imagined threats, "Dragons". A lot of dragons I have fought have not been battles over what people actually thought about me, but were battles over what I thought people thought about me. I've exhausted myself on things not even real.

Biblically, the devil comes in the symbolic form of a serpent trying to deceive us, and a roaring lion bringing condemning accusations against us. By far though, the scariest form of the devil from hell is that of the dragon. The beast that is mentioned thirteen times in the New Testament shows up in our lives as an overwhelming threat that wants to chew us up and spit us out. The thing about dragons....they are not real.

Just like the John Williams score playing when you go swimming in the river. Just because fear and strife are real, does not mean the threat is real. Knowing the truth makes you a dragon slayer. I refuse to waste my time and energy on battles that don't exist and in doing so I am better equipped to win the real thing.

John 8:32
Then you will know the truth, and the truth will set you free.

NOTES AND QUOTES

_____
_____
_____
_____

"Only when we are no longer afraid do we begin to live."
-Dorothy Thompson : American human rights activist.

IT'S GOOD TO GET A LITTLE HACKED OFF!

There's a stigma among cultural Christianity that the Brewer thinks is false. I call it the doctrine of "Niceism." It's the belief that being righteous means being nice all the time. This morning's sip from the Master's cup comes a little more caffeinated than usual.

I was reading this week about the Christian hostages that the Taliban has been torturing and murdering over the past few weeks. These 23 Christians from South Korea were on a mission's trip to encourage the church and help in any way possible, when they were kidnapped on July 19th.

Reports from the area show 18 of the 23 are women, and several of them are sick to the point of death. The kidnapping of these Christians, simply because they are Christians, is the largest abduction of foreigners in Afghanistan since the fall of the Taliban regime in 2001.

THE WORLD YAWNS

Nearly a dozen Taliban deadlines demanding the release of terrorist prisoners have passed since the Christians were abducted. Two male hostages have been killed so far with the latest death occurring last Monday. The first murder was of Pastor Bae Hyung-kyu, the 42-year-old leader of the kidnapped Koreans. He was found dead from gunshot wounds on July 25. His family said they will not hold a funeral before the remaining hostages return safely home. Can you imagine the grief these sweet people are going through?

The second murder was of 29-year-old Shim Sung-min. His bloodied corpse was found in the southern province of Ghazni, south of Kabul. The body was dumped in a field just off a main road, with his hands tied and bullet wounds to his head. From website reports he was an outstanding young man that wanted to make a difference in this messed up world. Nobody knows the terror that brother went through for being of a different race and a different religion; alone, in a foreign country surrounded by Muslim terrorists with no one there to help him or have mercy on him.

Taliban spokesman Qari Mohammad Yousuf said Wednesday the remaining 21 hostages are still alive, but that they will kill more if their demands are not met. The reports are the hostages are not being fed and there is not much telling what they have to endure.

WHAT ABOUT PARIS HILTON?

An official with the Institute on Religion and Democracy wonders where the outrage is over these murders and abductions of Christians. A lady named Faith McDonnell, the IRD's director, says the persecution of Christians does not seem to matter to national media. McDonnell is disturbed by the lack of information being broadcast, while Paris Hilton and Lindsey Lohan receive wall-to-wall coverage.

Additionally, she says, this situation shows the true face of radical Islam and the news is mostly reported as "foreigners" or "Koreans" are being murdered by "Terrorists" and not as "Christians" being murdered by "Islamic extremists" or "radical Muslims".

Because of the doctrine of niceism, Christians tend to fall in step with this crazy politically correct bunch of bologna. I know a lot of nice people that wouldn't lift a finger to help anybody. The world is very worried about not hurting the imagined feelings of one person while not giving a rip about real people that are really being tortured and really being shot in the head by very real bullets.

I wish that Christians and decent people of other religions and even non religions would get their priorities straight in what they get upset about. Anyone with any form of humanity in them, much less the love of God, should be outraged, sickened and grieved over what these Christians are going through. At the very least they should be interested.

Christians… I want to tell you something that you might not hear in traditional church services. God hasn't commanded you to be nice; he has commanded you to be full of life and full of the love of God. We are called salt and light to the world. Sometimes salt stings and sometimes light gives us a headache, but we are still supposed to preserve and overcome darkness for those around us. That might troublesome, but it's ok.

Matthew 10:34
"Don't think that I came to bring peace to the earth! I came to bring trouble, not peace." (Contemporary English Version)

NOTES and QUOTES

_____

_____

_____

_____

_____

"Victory is always possible for the person who refuses to stop fighting." – Napoleon Hill : American author who was one of the earliest producers of the modern genre of personal-success literature.

A TIME TRAVELERS PERSPECTIVE
OF CALVARY'S CROSS

This week's confession of a highly caffeinated Christian comes boldly perked with a seasonal blend. Palm Sunday, Good Friday, Easter Morning. It's not just a great time of year to sell little rabbits at the feed store, it's an amazing season to contemplate History's greatest hinge.

When I think about how Jesus lived, suffered, died and then slapped death in the face for me, I think about some things only a weirdo like me would think about. One of those things is Time Travel. Yes, time travel.

I would love to go back through time and actually witness Jesus in the flesh. Being a Christian I believe He was God made flesh, not just God pretending to be a man, so I tend to think other weird things too. Would I be able to talk to him since I don't speak Hebrew? Nobody actually spoke English 2000 years ago, much less Texan.

Maybe I would have to be a fly on a wall somehow and just observe. So on my time travel list of Jesus things to see would have to be, the feeding of the five thousand. Oh I would so want to see Jesus walking on the water and defending the woman caught in the act. What were you writing on the ground there, Jesus? So many things but more than all of that, even more than actually being in the house with the disciples when Jesus showed up after the resurrection, I would want to somehow be there the day he carried the cross.

Years ago I used to think about being in Jerusalem on that day and how I would love to be there just to encourage him somehow. I would love to give him a drink when he was so thirsty. I would love to clothe him when they tore his robe off of him. Anything to ease His pain or lighten his burden of what He was going through for my sake. If there was no way to do any of that, If I could just be one face in the hateful crowd that yelled back, "Thank you, Jesus!" You can do it Lord! It's not always going to be like this!"

This one day changes everything, Lord. Thank you sir, I love you sir!" Anything, so He wasn't so alone as He made that march for all of us.

So one night in prayer about ten years ago, I was praying and complaining to God about my lack of a time machine to do such a thing. "Yes, Lord I do plan to stop by the Alamo and make sure Davie Crocket knows you in his heart, but I want to come and love on you when you were hurting so bad."

In an instant, in a way like only God can, and in a way like is a little different for each of us, I felt God speak a word into my heart. "You already do and you have many times.", is what God said to me. A split second later, I was thinking about Matthew 25 and How Jesus said if we would give somebody who was a thirsty, a drink of water He would count it as if we did it to him. If we would visit folks in prison and clothe the naked and help hurting people he would count it as if we fed and clothed and helped Him when he needed it.

Come to find out I have done a lot of time traveling over the years. This last Saturday, me and my friends were able to give food and clothes away to over 700 people, and in that, I was able to encourage somebody who was hurt and feed somebody who was hungry. I never left the county or the current year but in the eyes of Jesus I was there with Him when he was hurting the most.

I can't go back through time like I would like to, but I get to live for Jesus right now in a way I shouldn't be able to. Happy resurrection day guys and God bless you in living out a life that proves He is Risen.

"I see the face of Jesus in every hurting person I take care of." Mother Theresa

NOTES and QUOTES

CHAPTER FOUR
FROM THE HEADLINES

I think God is speaking through literally everything around us. Romans chapter one, around verse twenty says that invisible things of God are clearly seen through things in creation. I love that verse.

Jesus went around pointing at common and extraordinary events in everyday life saying, "The Kingdom of Heaven is just like that!"

This next section is a series of columns I wrote on current events. Enjoy.

LIVING A RESCUED LIFE

The winter of 2009-2010 will long be remembered as the coldest and wettest ever. Not just here, but all over the world. I heard it was so cold in California, hitchhikers were holding up pictures of thumbs this year. OK, that's not very good, let's try this one: It was so cold two weeks ago, my grandmother's teeth were chattering — in the glass. Yes, that's better.

Thank you I am here all night. While I am not sure of how to tell a good, "It was so cold..." joke, I am sure of two things — it has been cold this winter, and Al Gore will blame it on global warming.

Winter in Warsaw
Three weeks ago, the temperature fell to -31 F in Poland and every river they have was frozen. The day the ice broke and the river began to flow again, also happened to be the day a full-

blood German Shepherd, Lucky we will call him, was crossing the ice through the city.

In a matter of moments, Lucky found himself floating on a small patch of ice and headed down river. People in town spotted the dog, and the fire department spent more than an hour trying to rescue Lucky. They gave up when the river moved faster and more ice broke free.

Two days later, the captain of a fishing boat spotted something strange in the middle of the Baltic Sea. "My crew saw a shape moving on the water and we immediately decided to get closer to check if it was a dog or maybe a seal relaxing on the ice," said Jan Joachim, senior officer aboard the Baltica. "As we got closer to the ice flow, we saw that it was a dog struggling not to fall into the water."

Ship engineer Adam Buczynski managed to scoop the dog off the ice and into an inflatable dinghy and wrapped him in a blanket. "He didn't even squeal," he said. Lucky had traveled more than 70 miles down-river and 18 miles out to sea. That makes him the Indiana Jones of German shepherds I think. The Brewer calls Lucky one blessed dog.

RESCUED AND SAVED

I think it is important for you and I, as Christians, to live lives that demonstrate how we have been rescued. You show me a person who has been rescued from certain death and I will show you somebody who loves life and wants to live it. Nobody comes out from under the rubble of a collapsed building with a bad attitude about what a privilege it is to be alive.

Just like that, nobody with a real revelation of what it means to be saved or rescued by Christ pines for the good ol' days and hates living today. I hope it is evident in our relationships and in the way we face the day, that you and I live the lives of rescued people. Jesus Christ has saved us in every way a person can be saved.

"For whoever calls on the name of the LORD shall be saved." — Romans 10:13

NOTES and QUOTES

MIRACLES AT WEDGEWOOD

"See You at the Pole" is a worldwide event that started in Burleson Texas. It's a student led prayer that happens around the flagpole at high schools all over the world. A day for the Christian kids to show their solidarity for each other and their witness to the rest of the school.

A lot of churches have special youth rallies the night of SYATP to celebrate Jesus and reach out to other kids. That is what was going on September 15th, 1999 at the Wedgwood Baptist church.

Larry Gene Ashbrook, a forty-seven year old jobless man known for violent rages and conspiracy writings, busted into that service yelling and cursing anything to do with Jesus. He pointed his pistol at bewildered teenagers and began pulling the trigger. A ten-minute rampage followed that would leave seven dead and seven more shot before he sent a bullet through his own brain.

GETTING THE WORLD'S ATTENTION

The unthinkable had happened. For the next several weeks, this single event would dominate anything that had to do with the media, particularly local media.

House Majority Leader Dick Armey issued a statement saying he "reacted with shock and horror". Calling it a tragic event in a «house of hope and love,» Gov. George W. Bush, along with other officials, expressed shock and dismay. President Clinton called Pastor Al Meredith and spoke to him personally, while Vice-President Gore spoke to him on "Larry King Live."

But for all the media, there was a lot that was not reported by the talking heads. Other things happened in the midst of those shootings that were not tragic at all, but in fact, miraculous.

MIRACLES IN THE MADNESS

Just before Ashbrook walked into the room, he shot out some windows right beside the children's playground. Every children's and preschool class was running late that night so nobody had made it to the playground yet.

In the midst of the shooting, Ashbrook lit a pipe bomb and threw it into the crowd of kids. Miraculously the bottom fell off and it didn't blow up the way it was supposed to, sparing the lives of many.

As the killer walked back and forth through the room shouting blasphemous obscenities and shooting at teenagers, a mother was desperately trying to force her mentally disabled daughter onto the floor. There was no way to calm her down and she made an easy target for the coward with the gun. Mary Beth Talley, a 17 year old who had ran into the room to warn every one of the shooter, saw the struggle and lay on top of the handicapped girl as Ashbrook went to kill her. Mary Beth heard the shot and then she felt a sharp sting as a bullet entered into her back.

Unlike other kids in the room, Mary Beth had scoliosis. This condition, a curse to so many, was in fact a blessing to this brave young lady. The curve in her spine directed the bullet away from her major organs and thus saved her life.

While most kids were wisely trying to protect themselves anyway they could, one young man with a troubled past and a biblical name sat up straight and bowed in prayer. "Lord, please let this end!" he prayed as bullets flew around him.

Jeremiah Neitz heard the shots; saw the slaughter, prayed the prayer, and then for some inexplicable reason, jumped to his feet and confronted Ashbrook. Not with his strong and muscular build, but with the love of God.

"Sir, what you need is Jesus Christ!" Jeremiah shouted as the gun was pointed at him.

"You can shoot me if you want," but I know where I am going. I am going to Heaven. How about you, sir?"

As mad as it made Ashbrook, the love of God in Jeremiah's voice shut the gunman down. He answered his question by sitting down in a pew, putting the pistol to his head and sending himself to eternity.

The people of that powerful church will tell you, "Yes, some of us have died because of our faith in Jesus." They will also tell you that they see the hand of God in the midst of the attack that came against them. They will say things like this: Though he fired 100 bullets into a crowd of over 400, only 14 were hit, an off-duty paramedic happened to be in the room and stabilized victims. None of the adults that died had any children. All seven victims were passionate and bold Christians.

The memorial service was aired live all over the world on CNN, including countries like Saudi Arabia, that do not allow the preaching of the Gospel within its borders. Because of the powerful word of God given in that service, people heard the Gospel and received Jesus that would have never otherwise had Jesus presented to them.

For every bullet fired against Christianity, millions of steps have been taken that move the cause of Christ forward. For every life lost through the shootings, thousands have been saved through the courage and testimony shown from the lives of those shot at. A lot more could be said, but I'll finish by quoting Paul as recorded in Romans 1:8....

"I thank my God through Jesus Christ for all of you, because your faith is being reported all over the world."

NOTES AND QUOTES

"There are only two ways to live your life. One is as though nothing is a miracle. The other is as though everything is a miracle." – Albert Einstein : Really smart guy

"Most if not all miracles are done in a big big mess." Troy Brewer : Not so much.

A TALE OF TWO KINGS

When James King Got up last Wednesday morning he woke up with a word and a mission. "God is going to help me find that little girl today."

Four days earlier, a little girl named Nadia Bloom, had gone missing without a trace of evidence as to where she could be. When her bike and her helmet were found on the side of the street, everyone suspected the worst imaginable.

There were however endless miles of Florida swamp nearby and friends and family knew Nadia had mild autism and lived with Asperger's syndrome. It was possible she had wandered off and simply gotten lost. They hoped it was possible.

She had just read a book about an adventurous little girl who went through the wilderness taking pictures of wildlife. Nadia did have her camera that day. After three days of Alligator infested swamps though, there were very few who considered it a possibility she could be found alive.

"At this point, it would be a miracle." Authorities said.

MIRACLES HAPPEN

Some time in the afternoon, 911 received a phone call from a remote location in the swamp. It was James King.

"I have found the missing girl, Nadia...." he said.
"Wait...You're in contact with her now?" asked the dispatcher.

"Yes, I have her in my arms. She's fine."

What CBS would call, The miracle in the swamp, was soon broadcast throughout the world. Nadia was covered from head to toe in mosquito bites and she was severely dehydrated but she really was fine.

"If I never believed in miracles before, I do now." said the chief of police.

Twenty four hours later King was in New York City on every morning news show you can imagine. An awkward kind of guy who apparently does not wear socks, King sat in nice chairs, in front of huge cameras, holding a bible.

"God led me to her. He told me to recite Proverbs three and call out her name."

Trust in the LORD with all your heart and lean not on your own understanding; in all your ways acknowledge him, and he will direct your path. That's what I did and I found her. "

Nadia's dad said of his daughter's rescue: «I can't even describe it. Let's give the glory to God.»

I know another King who searches for and finds lost people. This King is also a miracle worker. This king is willing to go where no one else is willing to go to rescue the hurting and save the lost. This King is actually King over all Kings and I know him personally because I happen to be part of the family. His name is Jesus.

In whatever swamp you find yourself sinking in this week, The Brewer encourages you to call out to the only one who really can rescue and save. God bless you so much as you face life believing in miracles and looking forward to the impossible.

NOTES AND QUOTES

_____

_____

_____

_____

_____

_____

_____

_____

_____

_____

_____

_____

_____

_____

_____

_____

_____

_____

_____

_____

_____

_____

_____

_____

"Miracles are a retelling in small letters of the very same story which is written across the whole world in letters too large for some of us to see." – C.S. Lewis : Christian, writer and intellectual giant

LEAP OF FAITH

When the sun finally came up it proved to be a beautiful Tuesday morning. Cool fall air and not a cloud in the sky. The morning commute to downtown Manhattan seemed a little more pleasant than usual. Jonathan Briley walked into the World Trade Center that fateful day looking up as always. I think about him.

The son of a Baptist Pastor, Jonathan grew up working on his daddy's P.A. system. His interest in music and speaking eventually landed him a job at the famed restaurant Windows of the World as the sound engineer. Anytime there was a conference or a celebration, it was Jonathan's job to set up and run the sound equipment.

On September 11th, 2001, the restaurant was holding a breakfast for 16 members of the Waters Financial Technology Congress, and 71 other guests. It was a day Jonathan had to be there early. About 20 minutes after he arrived, American Airlines flight 11 slammed into the North Tower just a few stories beneath him.

Eating in that same restaurant was Alayne Gentul, 44, a senior vice-president of the Fiduciary Trust and mother of two. As the room began to fill up with smoke she called her husband.

"Smoke is coming in from everywhere, Jack." She labored to tell her husband. "Guys are breaking the windows."
"Honey, go to the stairs and get out of there."

"We can't," she responded, "it's too hot in the stairs. Like an oven."

CAMERAS AND HISTORY

So many terrible things happened that day we will not forget. Some, we will want to.

As the estimated 1000 people trapped on floors 100 through 107 began trying to move away from the inferno, New Yorkers looked up with their hands over their mouths.

A photojournalist named Richard Drew, lived close to the towers. Richard was already no stranger to history. He had been one of only four photographers in the room when Bobby Kennedy was assassinated nearly forty years earlier.

At 9:41 am, 56 minutes after the ordeal had started; Richard pointed his I-lens upward and caught a man falling. He took 12 pictures of Jonathan Briley as he plunged 1300 feet to Church Street below.

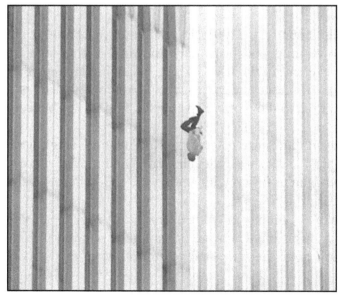

The Falling Man.

It's believed that Jonathan is the famous "falling man". The picture seen by millions throughout the world, of a person headed straight down completely vertical, almost casual.

His arms are by his side; his left leg is bent at the knee, and his white jacket billowing free against black pants. In the one famous picture he perfectly splits the towers. The north tower is to his left and the south tower to his right. It's an amazing photograph and one most of us wish we hadn't seen.

Jonathan was asthmatic and the toxic fumes forced him outside for almost an hour before he took flight. I think he thought it better to die flying then to die choking. In a place where every option had been taken away from him, he somehow mustered the courage to step out of the heat and into the hands of God.

In one of many interviews, Jonathan's elder sister, Gwendolyn, says: "When I first looked at the picture... and I saw it was a man like him, tall and slim, I said, 'If I didn't know any better, that could be Jonathan.'

When asked if his apparent jumping collided with their Christian theology she said something I think is quite brilliant. "Let me tell you how much Jonathan loved God. He trusted Him so much that he jumped 105 stories expecting God to catch him."

To Gwendolyn there was victory for her brother even in this tragedy…. especially in this tragedy.

No matter what terrible thing we are facing today, it pales compared to what Jonathan faced. Whatever tough decisions, I hope we have the courage to trust God when nothing else makes since. Jonathan Briley and his sister Gwendolyn preach to me. They help me.

I believe the next time we see Jonathan; he won't be falling at all…he'll be risen. Now that's a picture I want to see.

1 Corinthians 15:54
"So when this corruptible has put on incorruption, and this mortal has put on immortality, then shall be brought to pass the saying that is written: "Death is swallowed up in victory.""

NOTES AND QUOTES

_____
_____
_____
_____
_____
_____
_____
_____
_____
_____
_____
_____
_____
_____
_____
_____
_____

"Sometimes, your only available transportation is a leap of faith." -Margaret Shepard : Author, Artist & Calligrapher.

MIRACLE ON THE HUDSON

On Thursday afternoon, January 15th I had a chance to meet with my daughter Maegan for a short get-together. We try and do that a couple of times a week. It's like a dad date. Maegan is a stunningly beautiful, blond-headed, twenty two year old, nursing student who works at Plaza Medical. Among her many talents and qualities, her greatest flair is her God given ability to wrap her Daddy around her little finger.

She asked me what I thought about the day's news and said, "Isn't it wonderful?"

Now usually the words news and wonderful don't belong in the same sentence. That was the first I heard about flight 1549 and the crash landing everyone is calling Miracle on the Hudson.

If you are a regular reader of my column, you know by now I am a self-proclaimed Jesus Freak. You probably have also picked up that while I prefer the term cutting edge most would aptly call me off the wall. This week's confession of a highly caffeinated Christian blatantly states I am in all probability even worse than you thought.

I'm the kind of Christian the devil warned you about. I believe in miracles. I believe God isn't a symbol but an actual person and He speaks to all of us. I believe that while we live in a ruined world full of innumerable mess-ups, This God I'm talking about is prevailing in His goodness while being blamed for the bad. He's a really nice guy and I just love to hope in Him and look to Him.

I saw Him again last week. I think anybody with an eye to see, meaning people who wanted to see, saw God's goodness and heard a powerful message through our nations headlines on January 15th.

The themes being preached through this incredible event came power-packed with a word for you and yours. Let's take a look at some of them.

(1) This story is not about what went wrong but what went right.

Let me tell you I think this sentence belongs to you in 2009. Your story this year is not going to be about all the things going wrong but rather about the amazing things going right. It's like Isaiah 58:10 where it says your darkness will be like noonday. It's not about the darkness but about the brightness that's in it.

(2) What hasn't worked before worked perfectly this time.

We have all seen what happens when a jumbo jet tries to land in the water and typically it's a terrible disaster. I think what has hasn't worked before works for God's people this year. I am going after things again this year where I have failed before and believing this time it all works perfectly.

(3) Quick response is needed and cooler heads prevail.

Pilot "Sully" Sullenberger made quick and radical decisions that saved the lives of 155 people. This also should be our story this year. We should refuse to panic and make quicker decisions than ever before. Rapid response and appropriate actions will qualify us to get upgraded from a nobody to a hero in so many people's eyes.

(4) Sometimes you have to ditch the plane.

It's not about everything going perfectly, it's about a perfect outcome. There are certain victories you have to have this year and sometimes we get rid of things precious to us in order to achieve those amazing outcomes.

(5) Play books are being rewritten.

When they re-write the textbooks and the training manuals on what to do in that same scenario, they will follow the way pilot

Sullenberger did it. I think there are new ways of doing things that are better than how we have done things before. Don't be surprised if God has you blazing a few trails for others this year.

(6) Pay attention to the preflight safety announcements.

The instructions on how to safely exit a downed plane are being paid much more attention to after January 15th. The directions are not courtesy but specific instructions we had better take seriously if we want to be safe. (See Psalm 119:117, Proverbs 18:10, and Proverbs 29:25)

(7) The pilot and crew refuse attention and credit.

I think when God does miraculous things through us (we could all learn something from the pilot and crew of flight 1539) it's important for us to get out of the way, remain humble and not make it all about us. The idea is not to make Ministries famous but the good Lord all of us serve.

NOTES AND QUOTES

"Once you have tasted flight, you will forever walk the earth with your eyes turned skyward, for there you have been, and there you will always long to return." – Leonardo da Vinci : Painter, inventor, renaissance man.

"The reason birds can fly and we can't is simply because they have perfect faith, for to have faith is to have wings." – J.M. Barrie, Scottish Author and playwright of Peter Pan.

The Brewer and Sir Richard Branson
on his Private Island in the B.V.I.

CHAPTER FIVE
BEING BREWER

Most of the stories I tell have me in them. I am sure there is medication for that. But it's actually on purpose and there is a reason for it.

Like my childhood hero, Davey Crocket, I can spin a yarn. I have gotten better though they years because I have gotten better at seeing the story in the right now that I want to tell later on.

When I got sent to the ugly room in Cuba, I was thinking, Lord this is going to make a great story someday. Now the reason I have so many stories is because my life is so diverse and all of it is extreme. From Raising kids, being married, Pastoring a large growing church, Street outreaches, prison ministries, homeless outreaches, My Food bank, I am involved in six orphanages, I play guitar in bands, I have a radio show, I am typically out of the country 8 or 10 times a year and in all of that, there is a solid gold mine of relations, logistics, funny and tragic things. My life is really really big.

So sometimes when I set down on Monday mornings, with my perfect cup of coffee. Which has to be prefect. (Perfect cup, fresh ground strong, dark beans, two spoons of honey and a half inch of cream. Not milk but cream. I used to drink Soy and Splenda but the Soy Cranked up my estrogen and my boobies grew and I started crying all the time. To hell with that devil!)

I just stopped typing to make me a fresh pot. I'm back now.

Anyway, when I sit down and stare into my MAC, sometimes I just tell something cool that happened to me.

This Chapter is samplings from those kinds of columns and there were a lot of them through the years.

Here we go.

The Brewer and one of his homeless friends in Laticia Columbia on the Amazon River.

ON COFFEE AND COMMITMENT

So here I sit in the local Starbucks listening to the current sounds of coffee playing though the speakers. I casually sip on a cup of Pumpkin Spice Latte while downing my second Americano with soy and a Splenda. This is America's Crack house.

As I write notes, I glance around at my fellow java junkies. Like so many other Americans, the Brewer needs his daily fix to define the day. We also need to chase away the threatening menace of the non-caffeinated migraine. Most don't talk about it but my friends call it "the claw." For those of us who stay highly caffeinated, we know that the beast must be fed. If not, terrible retribution will be taken upon us like an invisible alien wrapping itself around our throbbing heads.

THE DAILY GRIND

My name really is Brewer and besides being fated to live up to my troublemaking name it is part of my DNA to consume large amounts of percolated pleasure. McDonalds should offer some kind of a "McCoffee" sandwich for guys like me. I imagine going to get a lap band and then surgically implanting a shunt to send coffee directly into my blood stream. I can invision moving to Costa Rica and growing my own beans off the side of erupting Mount Arenal. Oh, the things I will go through for just one serene bean. What else can I tell you; I love to drink coffee.

I love to love things. I do not want to be over compulsive but I like to play with the idea of it. There have been days when I've had too much and it caused me to be over stimulated and under motivated all at the same time. That's not good. But I do love-to-love things and not just coffee. To me it's kind of a loyalty thing. I'm big into loyalty. I love allegiance, commitment and sold out devotion. These are qualities and vices in people that really get my attention.

HOLY GROUNDS

As a pastor I see how messed up the whole ecclesiastical system can be and from a closer view than most. I love the church and when I say the church I mean the body of Christ; which are people of faith who really love Jesus and also love other people. But oh my goodness how I hate a bunch of the religious junk that we tend to operate in and pass off as no big deal. I believe Jesus Christ is totally anti-religion. He was 2000 years ago, and He still is today.

A lot of religious people will show you their degree and spout off on their "calling." They will boast on their talents and their qualifications about ministry. They look under their glasses at us lesser people in dignified snootiness on how blessed the rest of us are to have them contribute to the body of Christ gene pool.

I really don't think Jesus gives a rip about our talents or degrees. I think he qualifies people that are faithful; God loves people that are selflessly devoted. I don't think He cares about who's got the coolest collar, the closest parking space, the biggest hair or waves smoke on a rope. I do think He is looking to use people that will be committed. Even messed up people.

I think God loves faithfulness and loyalty. I really do. I also think He gets tired of our excuses for why so many of us run off the reservation. We run off morally, spiritually, ethically and just plain run off sometimes. (See proverbs 27:8)

He-Brews
So here I sit, a highly caffeinated Christian, musing on things that matter. Hoping I am on the same page as the biblical author. Believing that God thinks I'm funny and is crazy in love with me. Standing on the fact that it is by grace we are saved and not

of works lest any man should boast. And knowing for sure that a little bit of Jesus makes up for a whole lot of stupid.

I also pen this down as I spill a little more latte on my stained white shirt. Faithfulness, loyalty, commitment and devotion matter. If nobody else sees it, God sees it. Like an animal on the endangered species list, solid committed Christians are getting harder and harder to find. I encourage you in the Lord to keep yourself committed, even if it is only for an audience of one.

"Most men will proclaim every one his own goodness: but a faithful man who can find?" Proverbs 20:6

NOTES AND QUOTES

"Better to write for yourself and have no public, than to write for the public and have no self."– Cyril Connolly, English Author

"I meant what I said and I said what I meant." -- Theodor Seuss Geisel. A.K.A. Dr. Seuss, American Author, Artist and Poet.

WOODEN WONDER

When I was a kid, my mom married my step dad and I soon found myself spending a lot of time on his incredible farm, southwest of Alvarado. Back then, that whole area was what we indigenous folk call the boonies. I was scared Big-foot or Grandma Moses or what my great grandfather called "Raw head and bloody bones" was going to snatch me out of the shadows and haul me off to the creek bed.

Yes, the Brewer was a world class chicken.

At night, hundreds of coyotes would begin to sing a midnight song which I did not enjoy at all. The dad gum Peacock sounded like a woman yelling for help and the whole place just got spooky to me.

Now Dad's farm was a lot like the other farms around his place and often those farmers would spend a whole weekend trying to exterminate the local coyote population. In 1972, about a dozen families went to war with the vermin and shot what looked to me upwards to a hundred of these dogs in one grand hunt.

HANG 'EM HIGH

Now as a display of trophy and according to the myth that it would scare off other coyotes, all of those dead animals were nailed to the fence posts on the road. I will never forget trying to count them all as we drove into the farm and the number grew above eighty. -These rotting corpses of fur and teeth attracting a sky full of buzzards in the Texas summer heat. It was a terrible sight and it left quite an impression on me.

I am not six years old anymore and 37 years later, I've shot my own fair share of coyotes but I believe God let that one event make a verdict in me that I couldn't ignore for years to come. A Varmint verdict.

There was something disgusting and fascinating at the same time in such a spectacle. A symbol of hatred and triumph over them, nailed to a piece of wood and hung up for everybody to see.
Now I didn't have much between my ears in those days but The Spirit of the Lord touched a little boy's growing mind and I remember thinking somehow, the sight of that curse being hung up there, reminded me of Jesus hanging on the cross.

BLESSED BY A CURSE

I would later read what Paul said to the Galatians church as recorded in chapter three of that book. Christ redeemed us from the curse of the law by becoming a curse for us—for it is written, "Cursed is everyone who is hanged on a tree"— so that in Christ Jesus the blessing of Abraham might come to the Gentiles, so that we might receive the promised Spirit through faith.

In other words, at the cross Jesus became the curse and it was nailed down and hung up, so that we could be blessed. There is a huge mystery as to how all that works but the picture of this is so striking to me. That what was perfect became sinful and what was blessed became cursed so that a knucklehead named Troy Brewer could stand in a place called perfect and blessed.
There is something horrible and fascinating at the same time about the cross. It truly is a wooden wonder and I say "Thank You" to Jesus for it.

Max Lucado, a real writer and one a lot better than me, says it this way.

"It rests on the time line of history like a compelling diamond. It's tragedy summons all that suffer. It's absurdity attracts all critics. It's hope lures all searchers. My, what a piece of wood! History has idolized it. And despised it, gold plated it and burned it, worn it and trashed it. History has done everything to it but ignored it. That's the one option that the cross does not offer. No one can ignore it! You can't ignore a piece of lumber that suspends the greatest claim in history. A crucified carpenter claiming that he is God on earth! The cross. Its bottom line is sobering: if the account is true, it is history's hinge. Period. If not it's histories hoax."

NOTES AND QUOTES

_____
_____
_____
_____
_____
_____
_____
_____
_____
_____
_____
_____
_____
_____

"The world takes us to a silver screen on which flickering images of passion and romance play, and as we watch, the world says, 'This is love.' God takes us to the foot of a tree on which a naked and bloodied man hangs and says, 'This is love.'"--Josh Harris : Pastor, Writer, Speaker

BASEBALL AND BULLET PROOF BIBLES

Americana. It's a word related to our history and culture. When I think of Americana I tend to think of baseball, hotdogs and cowboy hats. So there I was, next to one of my teenagers, Luke, eating a hotdog and watching the Texas Rangers beat up on Kansas City.

We were sitting in the lower balcony on what is called "The home run porch" and for a brief while I actually believed I could catch a ball that was sent my way. I said a small prayer thinking how cool it would be if we actually got our hands on a real major league ball. I let Luke hear me pray it so I could give God credit for whatever gift came to us.

At the lead of the fourth inning, Michael Young hit a home run exactly to my seat. If you saw it on TV, I was the fat guy pushing people over trying to protect myself. There, on national Television and with my son watching, I screamed like a little girl and jumped a full two seats to left to try and get away from it. I didn't say a bad word but it was only because my lips didn't work and my teeth were clinched together.

The really awesome dad on the row in front of me (apparently a real man) held his glove up above my face and after catching it, handed the ball over to his slack jawed 9 year old.

Luke looked at me, I looked at Luke and we both busted out laughing. Lesson one on baseball night; be careful what you pray for, you might just get it. Lesson two; sometimes you just look stupid when you get what you pray for.

INCOMING!

One of the guys that I crawled all over was sitting next to my son. He was a 19 year old solider on leave from Iraq. We had already thanked him for his service and told him we would be praying for his safety. He said he was headed back to "the sandbox" on Monday.

I told him to keep his Bible with him and then asked him if he had heard about Private First Class Brendan Schweigart. He said no, so I told him the story I'm telling you now.

Brendan is a 22 year old from Andover, New York. He had his bible tucked in a pocket beneath his bulletproof shield when he was shot with a high-powered rifle while on a mission in Iraq. It saved his life by shielding the bullet from his heart.

According to reports, Schweigart told his mother, Kim Scott, that he always carried a Bible into battle. The Bible he was carrying was one he got at boot camp and there inside the actual book is the bullet that was meant to kill him. He still carries it with him today.

The sniper put bullets through his arm and another through his body but the one that was meant for his heart stopped somewhere past the book of psalms. Schweigart, who received a Purple Heart, has since been released from the hospital and is back on light duty. I think it's a great idea to keep your heart protected with God's word.

There is a bible with a bullet in it on display in the Alamo. It has a similar story with a different time and setting. I've looked at it through the glass in the long barracks on more than one occasion.

This week's sip from the master's cup comes with a little advice about protecting your heart. I have been really trying to wrap my head around what that might mean, lately. When that solider hid his bible under his vest he didn't know that it would cause him to dodge a bullet.

I think keeping God's word hidden in our heart causes us to dodge something much more lethal.

"I have hidden your word in my heart that I might not sin against you." Psalms 119:11

NOTE AND QUOTES

_____

_____

_____

_____

_____

_____

_____

_____

_____

_____

_____

_____

_____

_____

_____

_____

_____

_____

_____

_____

_____

The Brewer is also a mighty hunter of pigs.

THE CRITIC GETS CRITICIZED

This weeks' cup of Jehovah java comes with the idea of what it takes to get a fight started and it doesn't take much. These days it's either war or rumors of war, just as Jesus said it would be, so sit back and let this highly caffeinated Christian say a word about the intent of the confessions in these columns.

MY DAD IS BIGGER THAN YOURS

When William Wallace was headed out onto the battlefield field, his friend asked him where he was going? "I'm going to pick a fight," he replied. He didn't come there to look at the enemy, he came there to actually engage and accomplish something. He was the real deal and so should we be.

I am not here to pick a fight but I am here to be the real deal. Since my "idea" doesn't go along with that of others, sometimes I can peg a person's "cringe meter." That's not what I want to do, but just like coffee, a strong dose has its side effects.

My column is read by a lot of people in a bunch of different cities, these days including the hometown flagship here in Joshua, Texas. Because I am out there giving my opinions and views, I run the risk of ruffling the feathers of good and bad people alike.

ALL GOD'S FAULT

It's by design that I stir up trouble and rave on coffee…God's design. My name really is Brewer and brother Webster defines a "brewer" as one that brews or a troublemaker.

I don't like confrontation and friction but I have found that you are going to get a lot of it when you go against the grain and dare to be different; in other words authentic, genuine and real.

POST CARDS FROM HELL

For about a year now, I have begun to acquire a steady pouring of written response to what I write. Some of it, encouragement and appreciation but a lot of it is what I fondly call "hate mail." There is not a week that goes by that I don't get something from one camp or the other and I really enjoy reading both.

Some of my hate mail comes from sources you would imagine, such as people that have an absolute agenda against anything Christian. I have had two actual death threats in the past 4 years that are related to the "Fresh from the Brewer" and amazingly, both of them were from women. My Christian response is, "no weapon formed against me shall prosper." My Texan response is that there are some tough females at Open Door Ministries, and they will beat you down like a red headed stepchild.

THE ART OF WAR

Other such mail is from church folk that get their religious drawers in a wad because there is not a stained glass attached to my column. Others are from ministerial armchair quarterbacks that have no relevant ministry of their own, nor the guts to actually apply action to their faith, so they make a ministry out of trying to tear down others. They call themselves "Watchers on the Wall." I call them blessed...and other things depending on my disposition

PLAYING IT SAFE

I believe that the way of Jesus Christ is as Erwin McManus puts it, a barbaric and dangerous way. I think when God calls us he calls us to go out on a limb into risky, hazardous and vulnerable places. When we play it safe, we give up relevance and I am authentically afraid of spinning my wheels. I am not the lobster in the tank that just wants to blend. The passion within me wants to color outside of the lines to make a significant difference. I don't want to bury my coin as Jesus illustrated, I want to use it for all it is worth and to me that means not trying to be like everybody else.

So in trying to be funny and interesting to read for Christians and non-Christians alike, I run the risk of being called "an uneducated idiot not fit for print." In encouraging people to give their lives and hearts to Jesus Christ, I risk being called, "a typical right wing evangelical that preys on the stupid with the fairy tale notion of everlasting life." In not being churchy and using pop culture, I risk being called, "another pathetic example of worldliness in modern Christianity."

I have been called all of those things and much worse, but for me, it's proof that I am following the Lord into "all the world." Its barbaric, it's powerful, it's authentic and real but it is not safe, easy or religious foo-foo. We just have to be thick skinned enough to boldly be who God has called us to be long enough for God to get good mileage out of His investment in us.

So in the words of John the Revelator, I end this column like he summed up the bible, "May the grace of the Lord Jesus Christ be with you all, Amen." I really mean that for those that love me, and those that don't. To my critics and writers of hate mail, the words of the prophet Flo from Mel's dinner come to mind when I say, "Kiss my grits." And that to me is funny.

I knew they were scheming to hurt me so I sent messengers back with this: «I'm doing a great work; I can't come down. Why should the work come to a standstill just so I can come down to see you? Nehemiah 6:3 (The Message)

NOTES AND QUOTES

_____
_____
_____
_____
_____
_____
_____
_____
_____
_____
_____
_____
_____
_____
_____
_____
_____
_____
_____
_____
_____
_____

"When you're different, sometimes you don't see the millions of people who accept you for what you are. All you notice is the person who doesn't." -Jody Picoult

"I have spent a good many years since—too many, I think—being ashamed about what I write. I think I was forty before I realized that almost every writer of fiction or poetry who has ever published a line has been accused by someone of wasting his or her God-given talent. If you write (or paint or dance or sculpt or sing, I suppose), someone will try to make you feel lousy about it, that's all." - Stephen King

THE RIP OFF

When I was a kid I was a comic book freak. I loved Spiderman because of his good attitude and Conan the Barbarian because of his terrible attitude. I wanted to live life like Spiderman and conquer the world like Conan. It seemed reasonable to me.
I loved Marvel comics mostly because of the artists. I also loved Marvel because even if the character plot went stupid, a boy could count on the magic of the full-page ads. Those ads were as fantastic as the comics themselves and the items in them could be mailed directly to your mailbox.

There were Sea Monkeys — yes Sea Monkeys — hovercrafts and little machines you could buy that would help you counterfeit dollar bills. I loved it! Charles Atlas was willing to help me no longer be skinny and beat up mean people on the beach. I never bought his 15-minute trainer because I was never skinny and didn't live on the beach. However, I did take his advice and punched a bully in the face for making a remark about me. That bully promptly mopped the floor with my head in front of the entire seventh grade.

CATTLE KILLERS

There was also a really cool ant farm for sale. This was before fire ants invaded us and our Amdro killed all of the harvester ants, horny toads, tarantulas and jack rabbits. A big shout out to our state and federal government for handing out billions of pounds of Amdro to farmers in the early 80s. Feel the love.

I thought very seriously about buying the Venus flytrap plants and I always liked the zombie mask. But, there was one mail order item from the comic books that really stands out in my memory — the X-ray glasses. These glasses were advertised to help a young man full of testosterone actually see past the heavily clad ladies of our youth. I wondered why every kid didn't already have a pair and quickly came to the conclusion that it was because I was a visionary genius.

SNAIL MAIL

So in 1979, I saved up a $1.99 for my X-ray goggles, saved up another $5 for "shipping and handling" and carefully filled out the envelope so my messy writing would send my money to the right New Jersey address. I also dedicated my life to checking the mail every day for the next six weeks because if my mom found out I was trying to look through walls or cheerleader outfits, I would be dead.

Finally, after what seemed like an eternity, I got a very small package in the mail and a very lame pair of cardboard glasses. It was a scam. Who knew? I felt so cheated and stupid.

"You gotta be kidding me," I exclaimed while looking through the ridiculous rip off. The Brewer had his first taste of a world full of dishonest schemes. I mean you would think you could trust people helping little boys peer into Bank vault combinations.

MONEY BACK GUARANTEE

Thirty-one years later, I am painfully aware of rip offs and con artists and just plain lies. They compete for our attention and devotion at an unprecedented level these days. The one place I run to where I know I will not be ripped off or disappointed is hope in Jesus Christ. So I run to Jesus.

The proof of authenticity is not just in the book, but in the lives of all of us who love the Lord. We see miracles, live beyond what is reasonable and shoot for limitless possibilities. We love beyond our capacity and live beyond our means. We choose to be battleships instead of cruise ships and warrior poets full of life, love and joy.

It is just plain impossible for us to be the people we are without the reality of Jesus Christ in our lives. Besides all of that, I have been to Israel and stuck my head in the tomb — it really is empty. Jesus
Christ is risen from the dead and the life he gives to us is no rip off.

"They cried to You, and were delivered; They trusted in You, and were not ashamed." — Psalm 22:5

NOTES AND QUOTES

_____
_____
_____
_____
_____
_____
_____
_____
_____
_____
_____
_____

"Yesterday is history, tomorrow is a mystery, today is a gift of God, which is why we call it the present." – Bil Keane

"The world is indeed full of peril, and in it there are many dark places; but still there is much that is fair, and though in all lands love is now mingled with grief, it grows perhaps the greater." – J.R.R. Tolkien,

MY FLIGHT WAS THE BOMB

Fear and Loathing in San Antonio

Last week's mission trip to Mexico included a very rare plane trip back from Harlingen airport because I had a gig in Dallas on Saturday night. Yes, besides being a Pastor and writer, the Brewer moonlights as a rock star.

We had taken six thousand pairs of shoes to Brownsville, done a food outreach in the trash dumps of Matamoras Mexico and a really cool, hour long, live radio interview at K.I.R.T. in Mission Texas.

The team of people with us had to drive back but I opted to take two of my kids on a short plane trip to Love Field. I was supposed to do a sound check at the Hilton in Grapevine at two O'clock. Sounded like a great plan but of course there would be a story to tell.

At what was supposed to be a short layover in San Antonio, we were evacuated and had the hounds released on us as FBI agents combed for a bomb that had been reported to be on our very plane. I thought for a while that I was headed to Guantanamo Bay.

The Associated Press put it this way:

> SAN ANTONIO — About 100 passengers evacuated from a plane headed for Dallas today after San Antonio International Airport received a bomb threat, authorities said.
>
> The airport received several calls this morning saying a bomb was in Terminal One, airport spokesman David

Hebert said. Around 10:30 a.m., a caller referred specifically to the Dallas-bound flight.

Hebert declined to release the name of the airline, the San Antonio Express-News reported.

The passengers were evacuated and the plane was taken to a safe zone where airport police and a canine unit found nothing following a search, Hebert said.

The passengers were allowed to board again after a two-hour wait. The FBI is investigating, he said.

SNAKES ON A PLANE

I find it very interesting that there are no reports of the people they arrested even though I saw them taken off of the plane. We had just been cleared to leave San Antonio when they stopped the plane, reopened the door, and escorted one person out.

I think the airline handled the whole situation very well, however I would like to be fully reimbursed for my ruined underwear. I might be an awesome man of God but I'm a big fat chicken when it comes to airplanes. There is something about bombs at 39,000 Ft that make those complimentary pretzels run right through me.

By the grace of God and a bottle of Pepto, I was not only able to make my gig but actually play a set in front of four thousand people with all parts intact. It was a great night.

TEFLON COATED

There is really no telling what all God is protecting us from. I think it's worth noting that the Lord is taking care of us in different areas that we don't have a clue about. He is no doubt eliminating threats the way we lock cabinets and pick up sharp objects before our little ones even come into the room. I want to give God credit for all the ways He is protecting me in areas where I could never really give him credit for.

My kids are not sure what they think about their very first flight but I assured them it'll make a great story to tell the Grandkids someday. For that matter it might make for an interesting newspaper column.

I doubt it.

"He who dwells in the secret place of the Most High shall abide under the shadow of the Almighty. I will say of the LORD, "He is my refuge and my fortress; My God, in Him I will trust." Psalms 91: 1&2

NOTES AND QUOTES

_____
_____
_____
_____
_____
_____

In HAPPY MOMENTS   Praise God

In DIFFICULT MOMENTS   Seek God

In QUIET MOMENTS   Worship God

In PAINFUL MOMENTS   Trust God

In EVERY MOMENT   Thank God

LESSONS FROM THE SEPTIC TANK

Most folks in Texas live in an area like me where you have to have a septic tank. Often depending on how many teenage boys you have in the house, you have to call a reputable "environmental service" to come out with a giant pump and clean it out.

It's really not a pretty process but it's something which absolutely must be done and must be done right. The kind of people who own these businesses tend to be working class, family operations with lots of drive and generally a good sense of humor. They take the service they provide very seriously without taking themselves very seriously and I like that. This is what's behind the funny slogans you see on their trucks.

"A royal flush beats a full house" or "We're #1 in the #2 business". I saw a septic pumping truck in town that said something like "Caution: This truck is filled with political promises." Yes that's crude but it's really funny. Then again so is their business.

So once a year when my toilets back up, I make it a point to go outside and talk to the guy who makes my world a better place. About a month back, I called my favorite Yuck Truck and right on time he pulled up sounding like an M1 Abrams tank. We both stood over the concrete hole in my backyard and talked about life in general like only men can do.

FRIENDS IN LOW PLACES

Low and behold, this man was a guy I knew as a kid. We had seen each other at various parties back in what I refer to as my B.C. days. The last time I saw him I was wearing a Toga and cowboy boots singing with the Saint Pauli girl. Here we were twenty five years later standing over the same septic tank. "I worked in the oil field for a long time", he told me. "I got out of there because the only way you can be promoted in the oil field is to shake hands and to kiss butt and I'm not going to kiss anybody's butt." He made this speech of defiance as he looked me in the eye and pumped out my septic tank. I was thinking, what's wrong with this picture?

A few days later I couldn't quit thinking about what my friend had said and I prayerfully considered the importance of honoring the right people. Donald Trump knows the importance of strategic relationships and the kind of people he needs to be connected with. Rich people understand this principle and those of us that are typical Texans tend to reject it like a Boy George song.

For those of us in the Kingdom, we must learn the diplomacy of what it means to be an ambassador for Christ. This is not just behavior; it's a condition of the heart we must be willing to yield to. Honor produces upgrade. Honor brings opportunity. Honor brings favor. Let's be honorable people and partner with how God wants to upgrade our lives this year.

A man's gift makes room for him and brings him before great men.   Proverbs 18:16

NOTES _____
_____
_____
_____

The Brewer's just after meeting the King of Uganda. (Buganda) In Kampalla. This is what a man in a dress should look like.

KEEP THE CHANGE

The Brewer celebrated his 42nd Birthday last week. That's right, I'm half way to 84.

I am still a ways off from sinking my teeth into a steak and seeing them stay there but I am closer to sixty than twenty now. I know that the days are coming when an all-nighter means I didn't go to the bathroom once but that's not here yet, thank God.

What is here is the healthy realization that my days are numbered. At the same time I really feel I've got lots of life to live. I no longer feel bullet proof but do feel like I had better hurry up and do something cool. Forty-two is fun. Forty-two as a progressive Christian means I passionately believe in mortality and eternity at the same time. I think that's a good thing.

THE NEW THIRTY

I have never been afraid of getting older. I really enjoyed my teenage years, but my twenties were much better. As a teenager my life was full of snuff cans, football, shenanigans, girl friends and small town life. My twenties were full of marriage, ministry, having babies and learning how to live life in the big city.

My thirties turned out to be way better than my twenties and now I am full blown into my forties. So why would I not be optimistic? Leanna and I are about to celebrate twenty years of an incredible marriage, my oldest daughter is in college and the other three are in high school. It's a neat time, really. It's a time of closure for some things and wild possibilities for others things.

A really healthy attitude and a bi-product of victorious Christian living is the willingness to embrace transition. I think a blessed life is one that is growing and transforming. I also know I would not only be cursed but would be a curse to everyone around me if I was still the same person at 42 as I was at 21.

THE NEXT LEVEL

So transition is not about getting older, it's really about advancing. It's living from faith to faith or from everlasting to everlasting. It's learning how to hope for big things and remain confident through constantly having to deal with closure. It's about bitter/sweet goodbyes and hopeful/expectant new beginnings. One thing I am convinced at the end of 2008 is constant change is here to stay.

I am not going to change someday, I already have and I will again and again. So why fear it? It's a lot like the world we live in. We need not fear the world is going to change. It already has. You and I will live in a whole other world ten years from now, some for the better, a lot for the worse. So since we have no control over the direction of the world we might as well be determined to be better and better people. To be more and more hopeful, thankful and happier. I also want to be more and more useful to the Lord and more and valuable to those around me.

I love this life God has trusted me with. I don't really think I own anything; I'm just a steward. Part of being a faithful steward of the life I live means an adventurous willingness to embrace transition in growing, advancing and seeing how far the rabbit hole goes. So I think I'll keep the change.

A big Thank You goes out to everyone that plays such a key part in enriching my life, especially my 84-year-old Grandmother. After all these years, she is still a hottie and somehow still sees me as a very good boy. I love you, Nana. I am half way there to you in age, but a million years away in goodness of heart.

So teach us to number our days, that we may apply our hearts unto wisdom Psalm 90:12.

NOTES

"Someday, you will be old enough to start reading Fairy tales again." C.S. Lewis

SHOW OF FORCE

There was a day when a fight was only a fight. It wasn't an act of terrorism or a violent manifestation of suppressed feminine feelings. It was merely a couple of knuckleheads throwing down because boys used to do that sometimes.

The days of an honorable scrap have gone the way of disco. This used to be common place, meet-me-after-school event, including a hand shake afterwards is as likely to happen as the Ayatollah embracing Israel.

Today if a fight breaks out you can count on a mob or a gun. Should a young man miraculously survive, he might be mandated to spend years in therapy chasing his inner child. If the mob involves girls like it so often does today, and if they put it on You Tube, the young man will certainly need therapy. The possibility of his grandchildren watching a bunch of she-males beat him up is a legacy most don't want to pass down.

Should it happen at school, he'll get hauled off to Git-Mo and never seen again.

In my day, a fight wasn't that big of a deal.

FAST TIMES...

My mind goes back to the terrible eight-grade bully. This kid was spending his third year in the eighth grade and was the intellectual equivalent of Girls Gone Wild. He was a foot taller than all the rest of us and to me seemed undefeatable. After several months of being his piñata, my History teacher and two coaches took me aside. They closed the door and announced this was a clandestine meeting. It was years before I learned the word meant secret.

They said they were tired of seeing me get beat up by this Neanderthal. I had to fight back. My coach said I should hit him in the nose and surprise him. That day after school the bully found me and sure enough coach was watching the whole thing. To the bullies surprise I hit him right in the nose. To my surprise, up until that moment he had only been playing with me. The beating that followed is a classic in the annals of Joshua Middle School.

Coach broke it up but not before he got his terrible point across to me over and over again. I would feel his point for days to come.

Soon another clandestine meeting but this one with slaps on my back and encouragement. Why did you stop? Why didn't you keep hitting him? That was great! Troy you had him!

I wondered if they saw the same fight I had just been in. "You told me wrong!" I said through tears. One of the coaches looked at another and then my History teacher said, "Your right. Don't hit him in the nose, next time run up and hit him in the back of the head with a stick or a pipe or something."

That's when I knew these guys were crazy. I also knew there would be meeting after meeting until I had defeated this brute. Things have changed since the late seventies.

I don't want to go into details but the bottom line is by the end of the year I was holding my own and the middle school monster was finally thrown out. I didn't just grow in stature; I grew in confidence through every terrible battle. No longer afraid of being beat up, the bully didn't want to mess with me. My resistance discouraged him.

FAST FORWARD

Eighth grade was a long time ago for me but I carry something with me today from that season of my life. It's about being a warrior. Not that I am one. If I got in a fight today I would have to win in the first five seconds because around the 6th, I'm having an asthma attack.

I learned you don't become a warrior through one victorious battle; sometimes you become a warrior through a long succession of defeats. It's all about getting back up and going after victory again and again. If you do that, you discourage the enemy.

Victory grows with momentum. It's expediential. The Bible calls that faithfulness and faithfulness is all about persistence.

Now as a Christian and 28 years later I don't fight class bullies anymore. I've got a full time knock-down-drag-out going on between my own two ears. I battle darkness with light, lies with truth and overcome evil with God's goodness. I'm not worried about going to Heaven since Christ fought that battle for me. Basically, I'm all about Heaven invading this earth. If God can do that in me then He can do that through me.

HOLD FAST

You might have a history of messy ugliness, but God offers progression though every battle until that enemy is finally off of your radar. I love being a Christian. God doesn't measure success through every immediate implication but rather through the ultimate outcome.

I lost most of my battles to the middle school monster but ultimately won the war. Sometimes your greatest show of force is to remain in the fight. As a Christian I adopt the attitude of its ok to have lost certain battles in light of the ultimate outcome.

Your persistence and faithfulness to stay in the good fight of faith discourages the discourager. You're not messed up; you are simply on your way to being a warrior.

James 4:7
Submit yourselves, then, to God. Resist the devil, and he will flee from you.

NOTES AND QUOTES

_____
_____
_____
_____
_____
_____
_____
_____
_____
_____
_____
_____
_____
_____
_____
_____
_____
_____

"I would rather be a little nobody, then to be an evil somebody." – Abraham Lincoln

"If you're horrible to me, I'm going to write a song about it, and you won't like it. That's how I operate." – Taylor Swift

THE PERFECT DAY

When Leanna and I came back to our car last Tuesday, we first thought we were on the wrong street. No, my car was no longer there and somehow that dawning revelation affected my internal organs. It was a sick feeling.

We only had one day in San Francisco and having my rent-a-car stolen was not what I had planned. When I turned to Leanna she smiled and said, "That's what God invented insurance for," and we both hugged each other. I had a real adventure on my hands to see how we would get back to Sacramento.

In another minute or two I remembered my journal and Bible were in that car. My smile changing as my big fat lip poked out in a pout.

"Our books," I groaned.

Convinced my grandkids will read my journals; the loss began to sink in. Millions no doubt would some day have flocked to my own wing at the Smithsonian in hopes to glimpse the personal Bible of Troy Brewer. This theft was totally unacceptable.

Enter Homer. The 360-pound African American homeless brother with 5 layers of clothes, dreadlocks like the Predator and a sign around his neck that reads, "A cigarette would help."

"You think your car been stolen? It was...by the city." Homer started laughing and when he did he coughed up half a lung. His bright yellow teeth made me smile too because it was funny that he thought it was funny. So there we were, me laughing at him laughing at me. I saw the sign he pointed to with a worn out glove. It said no parking from 3-6. I had parked at the meter sometime around 2:30 and now it was 3:40. My car had been impounded.

We chatted with Homer for a while and had coffee together. He had squatted in Dallas, Austin and Fort Worth for a time. He resides now near the piers.

After 2.3 miles and a $20 ride with Amin the Ethiopian, we enter the environmentally friendly office of impounded cars. Amin was a neat guy and if you think about it, pray for him. He's here legally and trying his hardest to make things happen. 22 years old, full of promise and wanting to live the dream of an American. He said he had always wanted to see a rodeo.

I was seeing a side of San Francisco that's most folks don't. This was the park-in-a-no-parking-zone tour.

On the other side of bulletproof glass loaded with Obama stickers and something that said, "Send bread not bombs" sat Erica. Erica was the 5th daughter of Mexican immigrants. I learn things about people because my hillbilly accent triggers people to ask me where I'm from. She had family just south of San Antonio. Around us people screamed and protested but it was all blurry.

After a few minutes chit-chat she regretfully handed us a recycled piece of paper with a fine of $244.00 printed on it.

We began laughing again, the way men would laugh after they came out of Vietnam. I said, "C'mon Erica, help us. Were nice, your nice and nice people help each other."

She wrote down an address and said if we hurried to the courthouse we could catch a judge before five. We might get it dismissed.

We thanked her and went looking for our rented Mazda 6. There it was, with another ticket on the windshield for an additional

$70. What a wonderful racket this city has. I scanned the eco-friendly processed paper for any sign of mercy. With none there, we were driving around looking for the courthouse.

A few minutes later we ran up the courthouse steps past 2 men going through a mock gay marriage and looking for the right office because the judge leaves at five. The judge, who was Croatian, granted us the last hearing of the day. In a thick Eastern European accent he dismissed the $70 ticket but didn't the other. He had however, once bought an authentic pair of Cowboy Boots at DFW airport.

Thirty minutes later, Leanna and I caught the last boat out for a sunset cruise on the bay.

The guy running the boat was named Paul and had been painting his pots for this month's crab season. Paul had friends in Galveston that fish for shrimp. Paul was a neat guy.

My bride and me were on the back of the boat giggling about our whirlwind tour and about to go under the Golden Gate Bridge. We love this crazy journey. Paul picked up my IPhone and took a picture. The end of a perfect day.

You see, you can be mad over things gone wrong or you can have real justice in enjoying the ride anyway.

I think sometimes God gives us victory through slaying the giants in our lives. I love being a giant killer but I think other times we have victory when the giants don't matter.

It turned out to be one of the most romantic and loving evenings of our twenty-year marriage. Perfect weather, the sun going down into the ocean, a miracle moment.

I learned a long time ago, a move of God delayed is not a move of God denied. Sometimes the miraculous follows the ridiculous.

NOTES AND QUOTES

_____

_____

_____

_____

_____

_____

_____

_____

_____

_____

_____

_____

_____

_____

_____

_____

_____

_____

_____

_____

_____

_____

_____

_____

_____

How beautiful a day can be
When kindness touches it!
~George Elliston

A DIVINE RESPONSIBILITY

I was born on a glorious Tuesday back in 1966 in Fort Worth Texas. The date was December 6th. I don't know what was going on in Fort Worth that day, but I do know what was going on in Oxford Mississippi.

SHOWING YOUR COLORS

While I was screaming for milk and trying to get somebody to turn off the lights, 570 miles east of me, a young black man, a Christian, by the name of James Meredith, looked at his hands and saw the color red on them. He had just been shot.

James Meredith was an American Veteran who had served his country in the Air Force without so much a scratch on him. On the day I was born, he almost died at the hands of a white sniper who thought he should be killed for going to college.

He was the first African-American student admitted to the segregated University of Mississippi, a flashpoint in the American civil rights movement.

Motivated by his faith and his courageous sense of duty, James stood his ground, lived to be an old man and saw his son Joseph Meredith graduate from the University of Mississippi as the most outstanding doctoral student in the School of Business Administration.

Meredith said, "Nobody handpicked me...I believed, and believe now, that I have a Divine Responsibility..."

On that same day, 101 years earlier, The Thirteenth Amendment to the United States Constitution abolishing slavery and involuntary servitude, was officially adopted as Law.

A LOVE FOR JUSTICE

There seems to be some kind of hatred for slavery connected to the day I was born. I like that and I can see God in it. Lincoln once said, "Slavery is founded in the selfishness of man's nature, opposition to it, is his love of justice..."

My mixture of Texas and what I would call Kingdom culture demand many times I come to full froth and let myself get lathered up about injustice and just plain "what aint right."

I think it is part of my destiny to be a redemption fanatic. Jesus made me like that and I can't help it. I love freedom and hate control. So it just makes since that I would sometimes dabble and sometimes be completely dedicated to seeing people set free in every way they can be. Like the amazing James Meredith, you and I both have a Devine Responsibility.

ABOLITION AND REDEMPTION

Because of that, through the years I have had the privilege of buying Human beings, paying off debt and seeing lives transformed in ways that are truly privileged.

In the late 90's I met with a very addicted rock star named Layne Staley and an hyperactive crazy man named Perry Ferrell who both were known by millions for music but were trying hard to help enslaved people in East Africa. We spent the day at a restaurant in San Antonio with a hand full of abolitionist activists. When the day was done, we arranged for the payment of what might have been hundreds of families literally enslaved in southern Sudan because they were Christians in a Muslim land. These kinds of things are done by people every day all over the world and you probably don't even know about it.

For more than 15 years I teamed up with several hundred people and we went into the trash dumps of Mexico, paying off the debt of the people who were forced to work and live there. More than 500 people from Joshua Texas made the trek throughout the years and we literally bought whole families at a time. Some who had been born in the trash dumps because their parents owed the Cartel money somehow.

I bought two little Nicaraguan girls, barely teenagers, who were offered to me in Costa Rica because the woman who sold them to me assumed I was a sexual tourist. After all, I was a middle aged American in the slums and that's what they are doing all over the world. Those two little girls grew up protected in an orphanage of a friend of mine, set free from Sex Trafficking.

I could go on and tell you a bunch of other stories but the bottom line is that nothing, and I mean absolutely nothing, changes and transforms a person's life like being bought from the hopeless clutches of slavery. There is no bigger game changer than redemption.

So you have to pardon me and my Christian friends for being excited about being Christians. I know it might get on your nerves and sometimes we just aren't smart about how we are always talking about Jesus. Jesus this...Jesus that. We just can't help it because a bunch of us actually get it that we have been bought with a price. So yeah, we get a little wound up about the possibility of you getting set free too.

So I raise my cup of coffee to the 13th amendment, James Meredith and the day I was born ...and born again.

Let the redeemed of the Lord say so, Whom He has redeemed from the hand of the enemy. Psalms 107:2

The next picture is one of my all time favorite moments caught on film. We were going house to house and mud hut to mud hut taking food and clothes to unsuspecting people in Uganda.

This sweet lady and her 3 kids brought the only piece of furniture they had, a mat, to lay on the ground for all of us to kneel on. We had a little Jesus-Fest right there together that day.

The Brewer, suffering for Jesus in Jamaica 2014.

CHAPTER SIX
ODDS AND ENDS

My last Chapter is a segment of just weirdo musings. This by the way is me and my world famous atomic Rockstar pet chicken. "HIPPY"

HOLD YOUR NOSE!

The smell of Coffee in the morning puts the Brewer in a good mood. I love the smell of coffee. I like the smell of lots of things. Leather, the Sunday pork roast, a brand new car.

Smell is a big deal. It's the only sense you have that extends directly into your brain. It's a key component to our moods, memory and appetite.

Your nose is a truly remarkable structure. When a nose functions the right way, it can help us detect as many as 2,000 different scents. It also conditions the air we breathe. We inhale about 17,000 times a day, moving some 300 cubic feet of air through our nostrils every 24 hours.

That's a lot of nose business. That snout of yours has to clean, humidify and in a fraction of a second, warm or cool the air you breathe to match your body temperature.

A scent, fragrance, or aroma also have a powerful effect on our emotions that help transform the way we feel. Specific smells suppress appetite, reduce stress, revitalize and energize, even promote physical attractiveness. I know I certainly become much better looking when I throw on some Old Spice.

The thing about smell is that it can do the opposite as well. A bad smell can put you in a bad mood or flat wear you out.

KING JAMES

You might know the name King James because of the famous English translation of the Bible. What you might not know is that he was a character that didn't care to live a life reflecting the Bible he had commissioned. His very interesting life as King of

England is something worth looking at. Though a promiscuous homosexual, he married Anne of Denmark and had seven children who survived beyond birth.

He himself survived the Guy Fawks gunpowder plot but none of those things are really what King James was famous for. King James suffered from a terrible fear called aqua phobia and he never took a single bath his entire life. Those around him suffered the smell of a King who refused to put water on his body. He was a presence to be reckoned with and when he came into a room everyone knew it.

There's nothing worse than somebody that reeks from a major malfunction of personal hygiene.

THE STINK IN THE BIG BEND

Big Bend National Park is an amazing place and that area was the last frontier for the lower forty-eight.

When people in the rest of the United States were voting for Roosevelt and driving the Model T, Texans in the big bend were enduring Apache Indian raids on ranches and dealing with bandits robbing their banks.

Extremely eccentric places tend to attract eclectic characters. Bobcat Carter lived at the Permission Gap entrance to the National Park. He devoutly preached to all that, «Cleanliness is next to Godliness. A true gentleman should bathe at least once every seven years. I do!»

People say you could smell him a mile away. He ate skunk stew, drank from a pregnant horses udder and poisoned prairie dog villages for a living. He would turn back flips along the road just to stop visitors for a chat.

After more than a hundred years old, he was taken to a hospital in Alpine. In terrible protest they removed his filthy rags and scrubbed his nasty body. "Don't let them kill me!" He cried, as black water splashed across his elderly form.

Three days later Bobcat Carter died, apparently the victim of pneumonia. The bath had actually killed him.

THE SMELL OF SUCCESS

When you can't see something or feel something, you can still identify it if you can smell it. The sense of smell is all about discernment. I think if there is anything Christianity needs today is a strong sense of spiritual discernment. A lot of things feel right and look right but you can just tell they are not because of your spiritual "knower". The ability to be able to identify what is God and what is not. What is life and what's not something that brings life?

Furthermore the people around us should be able to sense something different about Christians. We ought to be so full of life that people around us can smell it on us.

The Christian church is metaphorically called the body of Christ. This body is really attractive when we are properly joined with Christ the head. I think one of the reasons why Christianity is so unattractive to so many people is because too many of us are bodies that have become unattached to Christ as our head. After it's all said and done, a headless body is good for nothing but lying around and stinking up the place.

Philippians 4:18b
"...the gifts you sent. They are a fragrant offering, an acceptable sacrifice, pleasing to God."

NOTES AND QUOTES

"Mostly because of my bad personal hygiene, they asked me to work the night shift at Atari." -Steve Jobs

A FUNNY THING HAPPENED ONE SUNDAY

This week's confession from a highly caffeinated Christian comes brewed with controversial observations on laughter.

WHERE THERE IS FIRE...

Rules are not funny to me but rules can keep you out of a world of hurt. If there is a rule, it is probably because something happened that somebody else doesn't ever want to happen again. For example, we have "No Smoking" signs at the entrance of our church because Open Door Ministries tends to attract the "Marlboro man" to our services. Rather than run him off, we just want to keep him from firing one up during the announcements. You might think you don't have to ask people to refrain from smoking at church but we have discovered signs are required in Johnson County.

JESUS WON'T YOU LIGHT HIS FIRE

There is a good reason why we have one person in charge of calling the prayer chain instead of just handing out the long list of phone numbers for our church's prayer warriors. We used to provide those phone numbers until one lady called through the entire church and asked us to pray for her husband's apparent erectile dysfunction and asked that "the spirit would move" at around 10:00 pm on Friday.

When her poor husband found out, he called through the same list insisting that there was no physical problem and that he would probably be asleep by 10:00 on Friday anyway. We don't give out those numbers anymore.

FIRE IN THE SKY

When I was young, I used to let people in the crowd give testimonies but I quit handing the microphone over when one woman shocked the congregation in 1998. Her testimony was that she was in her back pasture when the "Mother Ship" landed not far from where she was standing. She wasn't sure if they were angels or "fire aliens" but something came out and ran her back into the house. I don't hand over the microphone anymore.

If you have church long enough, especially if you are an outreach church, you're going to see things that you never thought would happen in a million years. Things that make you want to bust out laughing and make others want to run off crying.

GUN FIRE

The first time I preached in Matomoros Mexico, Pastor Gene Izaguira told me the Mafioso had just warned him not to be preaching anymore to their drug runners because too many had been converted to Christ. When he refused, the bad guys told Gene they would assassinate him behind his pulpit on that very night. Mind you, this was the first night I showed up down there to preach.

"So if somebody walks in and shoots you bro," he said with his hand on my shoulder, "it's nothing against you personally."

That night an armed gunman was stopped at the door by the 2 new converts who had not yet learned the doctrine of self-control. Forrest Griffin would have been proud of their "ground and pound" technique. In the midst of the brutal beating, that young man decided to give his life to the Lord and is a big part of Gene's church to this day. That was my first time down there and I've been back more than 60 times since. How can you not love a church like that?

FIRE FROM HEAVEN

Just a few months ago, my band was playing at a motorcycle church in Chico, Texas. At the end of the service, a worn out practitioner came forward in his leather and long hair asking for prayer about his hearing. "I'm real scared and I need a miracle", he said to the Pastor.

We laid hands on him and the Man of God broke out some olive oil and put it on both his ears. They whole prayer team rebuked the devil, shouted at Heaven and proclaimed a miracle healing as our band played upbeat worship as backup. After a good ten minutes of lively scripture quoting and charismatic breakthrough, the team got quiet and the Pastor asked him how his hearing was? The man, with a confused look and oil dripping off both ears stated, "perfect, I can hear perfectly".

Just as praise began to bust out in the church, the man interrupted, "my ears are not the problem! It's tomorrow's court hearing I'm worried about." I laughed so hard I had to leave the room.

A big part of having real victory in your life is being led by God to know what you should and should not take too seriously. If you are all wrapped up in yourself, you're a gift everybody else could do without. I double-dog-dare you to ask the Lord to give you a heart that loves to laugh. After all, that's His heart too.

"He will yet fill your mouth with laughter and your lips with shouts of joy." Job 8:21

NOTES AND QUOTES

THE DEADLIEST CATCH

Most folks in the world wouldn't know anything about Dutch Harbor, Alaska or its small town called Unalaska, Alaska. But now millions tune in every week and click the worldwide waste of time looking for anything they can find. Dutch Harbor is the home base for the fisherman documented through a hit TV show called Deadliest Catch.

The weekly series on the discovery channel follows eight to ten crab fishing boats and their crews throughout the dangerous crab fishing seasons. The King Crab they fish for, frequently called «red crab» or «red gold» only comes to the surface after 16 hour work days in what could be lethal conditions.
The fourth season just started last week and the Brewer is a big fan. My favorite boat is the Time Bandit but I also like Captain Sig Hansen's team of the Northwestern. I don't get to watch every episode but I catch one or two a month and love it every time.

THE PERILS OF FISHING

Last year the producers of the show were able to document the rescue of a man that fell off his boat and was miraculously rescued by the crew on the Time Bandit. Others have not been so fortunate. A boat featured in season one, The Big Valley, sank at the start of the 2005 season; five of the six crew died. It was a terrible, tragic loss.

Whatever the reason, the risk and the consequences of error or just being in the Bering Sea in January, are absolutely real. I would like to think I could "man up" and do that but I know in my heart I couldn't. I'm too old and too fat and I get seasick way too easy. I love to fish and I love adventure but I have learned you don't have to move to Dutch Harbor for dangerous adventures in fishing.

SLEEPS WITH FISHES

Through the years, there have been all kinds of documented reports of how serious fishing can be. From The Perfect Storm to Moby Dick, there are some whoppers out there.

There is a famous story about a guy named Marshall Jenkins, surviving after being ingested by a huge whale in the South Seas during the fall of 1771. As the Boston Post Boy newspaper reported on October 14, 1771, a whaling vessel from the port of Edgartown, Massachusetts harpooned a whale that turned and attacked its pursuers.

First, the whale bit into one of the boats, then swallowed Jenkins and submerged. When the enormous whale finally rose again to the surface, the whale vomited Jenkins onto the floating wreckage of the broken harpoon boat, «much bruised but not seriously injured.» Jonah, eat your heart out.

FISHING FOR MEN

As dangerous as it is to fish for sea creatures, there are about 40 countries in this world where it is much more dangerous to be a Christian and fish for men.

The metaphor of fishing was used by Jesus himself and in a lot of places in the world; a Christian is still the deadliest catch. People don't realize that while places like Saudi Arabia are funding millions to build Mosques all over Europe, they will execute anyone trying to build a church in Saudi Arabia.

Fishing, especially for Christians, is still perilous.

One of my favorite fish stories is about a guy named Wally Magdanga. He was arrested in Saudi Arabia for being the Pastor of one of the largest underground Christian Churches in the land of Mecca.

The most wanted man to the Saudi Government's secret police was a Pastor that dared to print tracts with Bible verses. He had the audacity to give people the good news of Jesus Christ in a country controlled by Muslims. Something that is never permitted in a country controlled by Muslims and this of all places the home of Mecca.

The day they tore down his front door, assaulted his wife and children and arrested all of them is a day Pastor Wally will never forget. Sitting in the back seat of a secret policeman's car, about to be taken off and tortured, the officer in the front seat turned around smiling.

"I have finally caught the big fish" He gloated through yellow teeth

"No," Pastor Wally replied, "You have only caught a little fisherman."

ILLEGAL FISHING

There are at least 40 nations in the world right now where Christians are routinely imprisoned, tortured and even executed.

The worst place for Christian persecution in the world is North Korea, according to Open Doors' 2008 World Watch List. The annual country persecution list ranked North Korea in the No 1 spot for the sixth year in a row.

In second place behind North Korea is the kingdom of Saudi Arabia where fundamentalist Wahabbi Islam dominates society and oppresses believers. Under the Kingdom's strict interpretation of Islamic law, apostasy (conversion to another religion) is still punishable by death.

The 2008 top ten worst offenders list for atrocities against Christians looks like this. 1. North Korea 2. Saudi Arabia 3. Iran 4. Maldives 5. Bhutan 6. Yemen 7. Afghanistan 8. Laos 9. Uzbekistan 10. China

I encourage you to get involved, write a letter and say a prayer for our persecuted brothers and sisters. Visit www.persecution.com and www.persecution.org for more information.

NOTES AND QUOTES

_____
_____
_____
_____
_____
_____
_____
_____
_____
_____
_____
_____
_____
_____

"It was strictly forbidden to preach to other prisoners. It was understood that whoever was caught doing this received a severe beating. A number of us decided to pay the price for the privilege of preaching, so we accepted their [the communists'] terms. It was a deal; we preached and they beat us. We were happy preaching. They were happy beating us, so everyone was happy." – Richard Wurmbrand: Christian, Jew, Author

WHY I LIKE IKE

When Pioneer 11 swept by the planet Jupiter in December 1974, the little spacecraft did something amazing for all of us. Like a kid running past a playground with a low-tech cell phone, the little metal gadget took a dozen close-up pictures on it's way to parts unknown.

It took a long time for NASA to download and clear up those photos, six months as a matter of fact, (and you think your computer is slow) but in May of 75, NASA released part of its planetary portfolio. People threw babies in the air.

The photographs stunned the world with the most detailed view yet of Jupiter's great red spot. A hurricane-like storm as big as our planet with components beyond comprehension. It turns out the lethal mixture of things like ammonia, methane and even liquid metals flying around at speeds of 400 miles an hour make for really cool pictures.

It's scary but you can't help but look at it. It's something really ugly that's amazingly photogenic. Reminds me of Keith Richards and the Rolling Stones.

Hurricane Ike is nothing like the Great Red Spot but it's a terrible storm nevertheless. As it barrels down upon our beloved Texas, folks down south batten the hatches and buy stock in Home Depot.

I was recently in Brownsville after Hurricane Wilma made land fall on July 23rd. I saw the aftermath of what a weak category 2 hurricane does. Man what a mess. Now twice in the same season, the Texas coastline suffers a headache at best and a killer at worst. It's a good time for prayer warriors to sharpen their swords on behalf of those overwhelmed by Ike's devastating destruction.

One of the cities that have been affected greatly by both hurricanes is the stunningly beautiful Corpus Christi. The name Corpus Christi means the Body of Christ. The Brewer does not believe this is a coincidence. I think God is speaking to us Christians.

Ladies and gentlemen, buckle your seatbelts.

There are all kinds of thought on the voice of the Lord but I think God talks through anything and everything. Romans 1:20 says that the hidden things of God are clearly seen through the things around us or the things that are made. Some of the deepest truths I have ever received from God have been through life messages. Some of the greatest revelations have been through things my little kids have said or in everyday situations.

We preachers have very little influence in reaching the masses. I don't think God is scared one bit to use the headlines to get a point across. I even believe Hollywood is the Jackass; God will use most to speak to this generation. That's another story.

Jesus himself went around pointing at common events in people's lives and revealed deep spiritual truths saying, "The Kingdom of heaven is just like that!"

Psalms 29 says that the voice of God is not limited to any one way of delivering His word.

The voice of the LORD is upon the waters: the God of glory thundereth: the LORD is upon many waters. In this case, I think the voice of God might literally be upon these waters.

Now you probably think I'm going to tell you this is a word of judgment because of the disaster involved. I don't think God is fixated on judgment like a lot of my friends in the Christian community are. I think that's what the cross was for. It seems to me, many times the greatest of the goodness of God is revealed in the biggest of messes. That's the Jesus I know.

The name Ike is a Hebrew word associated with the understanding of laughter. Could it be that God would have an encouraging word of laughter in the midst of such hardship? You bet He does. The idea of Biblical laughter is not so much about getting the jollies as much as it is about having confidence in an overwhelming circumstance. In the book of Job, the Bible says God will make us to laugh at our enemies. It's a word of confidence. Now is not the time for you to back up or shut down. Ike has changed your weather.

It's also worth noting that Ike is remembered in America as a war hero and the 34th President of the United States. 34 is the Biblical number for miracles. From turning the water into wine to healing the ear of Malchus, the Bible records 34 pre-resurrection miracles of Jesus.

The point is that there is a very real change in the season for Corpus Christi and it's got Ike and 34 all over. If you want to see God speaking in this I think you can and if you want to receive it, I think you can. The body of Christ needs real war heroes to rise up and believe God for his manifest power in these difficult days. Hurricane Dolly blew through Corpus and Padre Island six weeks ago. Dolly is a feminine form of the word sorrow. Dolly means Sorrow, Ike means Laughter. The body of Christ has a choice to make in the midst of our storms. I like Ike.

NOTES AND QUOTES

_____
_____
_____
_____
_____
_____
_____
_____
_____
_____
_____
_____
_____
_____
_____
_____
_____

"I was born in a crossfire hurricane. " -Keith Richards : Musician, songwriter, Actor, Rock Star

"When You choose life, You break the heart of blind mechanical fate and cause God to stand and applaud." Troy Brewer : Rock Star Pastor

"Look deep into Nature and then you will understand everything better." Rock Star Physicist

"The Voice of the Lord is upon the waters, upon the many waters.." David : Rock Star King of Israel

"The Kingdom of heaven is just like that!" Jesus Christ : The single greatest person living in the universe. And yes, He rocks the Stars.

*Aaron Copeland from The Casey Donahue Band and The Brewer
with his favorite Fender 'Big Tex".*

THE LAST DROP OF A WORD

Well that just about does it. With over 500 columns to choose from, I no doubt left some of the best ones out. That's the thing about writing books, once it's writ, its writ.

I close this by saying, and I wish you could hear me say it in this little room in Costa Rica, "STAY INSPIRED!"

Remain full of Passion and be constantly looking through everything around you for the heart of that amazing person who makes your baby leap.

Seek him, find Him and celebrate Him every time you find Him in something new.

Someday You and I will live together in the same place with the King of Kings and we will look back into this day and wish we had demonstrated, sought after and loved Jesus even more.

Go after the heart of God, my friend!
Seek Him in off-the-wall, out-of-the-box kinds of ways and find him in extraordinarily unique ways that only belong to you!

He really wants you to do that and is inviting you there in a way that is completely exclusive.

Be brave, be strong & Have Fun.

Troy.

THANK YOU'S AND THAT KIND OF THING

PAULA LEDBETTER
I started writing Fresh From The Brewer because Paula called up to the Joshua Star and said, "Hey, my Pastor is an awesome writer and you should print something he writes.

She informed me that same afternoon that I needed to go write something worth reading and that's how all this started. Thank You Paula.

THE STAR GROUP NEWSPAPERS
I have become good friends with Brian Porter through the years, who edits all of the Star Group Newspapers. Even while on this trip in Costa Rica to finish this book, he has consistently bugged me with texted quotation from True Grit and other John Wayne films.

My Partnership with you is greatly Appreciated.

DEBBIE CALDWELL
Thank you Debbie for taking my scribblings and inklings and rantings and working your magic.
Love you!

JACOB DUKE
Thank you for being my squire. A squirrel squire who jumps through my ever increasing hoops to assist me. thanks for helping me with this book and all things Brewer.

SPARKWORLDWIDE.ORG
The sales of this and all of my books goes toward the efforts of SPARK's on- going battle to serve Protect And Raise vulnerable Kids throughout the world.

Because of that, you graciously foot the bill for my printing costs and I am so grateful. I can't express how proud I am to be a part of this amazing organization.

OPENDOOR CHURCH
Thank you for putting up with a Pastor who is a goer and not just a sender. Off-the-wall-out-of-the-box-and-in-your-face. You are the coolest church ever. Love you!

THE BREWER BUNCH
Maegan, Ben, Luke, Rhema, JC, Brandi, Patrick, Barrett and Sophie. I Love you and thank God for you. The only reason I can write so much is because I have peace in my heart and satisfaction in my soul over who you are to each other, the Kingdom and to me. Love you and appreciate you.

LEANNA BREWER
Thank you for not being jealous of all the time I spend with those other women, -the computer, the radio, the church, and that crazy wench called the world.

You make me ready to run back home to you every time. Love you and happy 25th anniversary, Lady.

*Leanna and Troy Brewer with some of their kids
in Uganda, East Africa 2014.
www.sparkworldwide.org*

How to Contact Troy Brewer

To find out more about Troy Brewer, Support his ministry or listen to hundreds of hours of his sermons, you can go to

www.opendoorexperience.com
The Website of OpenDoor Church in Burleson Texas

www.sparkworldwide.org
The Website of Troy and Leanna's orphan ministry

EMAIL: troybrewer@me.com
Snail Mail : PO BOX 1349; JOSHUA TX, 76058

For bookings, conferences etc, contact him through Email or call OpenDoor Church directly at
817-295-7671

More books by this Author

Miracles With A Message
Aventine Press 2002
Miracles with a message Is an amazing collection of modern day miracles interwoven with power packed, biblical wisdom that will build up your faith and encourage your heart. These chapters include, Miracle at Wedgewood: As a lunatic killer shot up a church in Ft Worth, Texas, the hand of God was leaving proof that He is still in the protecting business. Perfect Timing: A prisoner's prayer for a miracle caused God to deliver the very next day and of all places at The Ballpark In Arlington! Flight 191: On August 2, 1985 rescue workers frantically went through the wreckage of a crashed commercial airliner at DFW airport. Hours before that plane went down, God did an amazing miracle to keep a little girl from boarding that plane. These stories and many more will increase your faith, encourage your heart and advance your trust in the loving God we serve. These are not just Miracles; these are miracles with a message.

Soul Invasion
Aventine Press 2003
The battle for the brain is on and you can win this battle! It would be silly to think that God would want you to have victory throughout your life without winning the everyday battles between your two ears. If you are really serious about your walk with God, this sometimes funny, and sometimes somber group of tactics will help you Sober up in correcting very real mental malfunctions. SOUL INVASION will teach you effective Biblical strategies including How to "armor up" in your thinking How to deal with Haters How to Spiritually "arrest" your thoughts before they progress & accelerate Jesus driven thinking that helps and heals Confronting unhealthy mindsets in 11 common but very different arenas and much much more! This Book will

bring you peace, and in knowing the Truth the Truth will set you free.

Fresh From The Brewer: Sips of Wisdom From the Carpenter's Cup
Aventine Press 2005
Pastor Troy Brewer brings you a delightful collection of his newspaper columns from Johnson County, Texas. These incredible stories & things observed come mixed in his unique blend of powerful spiritual insight, & witty southern charm. Wisdom from the carpenter's cup was meant to be slowly sipped on and then quickly acted upon. Like a good cup of gourmet coffee you have to savor it and cherish it until it warms you like a thick blanket in the cold of winter. A timeless testament to the power of God's voice through every day events, this collection is sure to encourage, support, comfort and, most of all, inspire all readers for years to come. This book is one cup that you won't want to put down.

Fresh From the Brewer Volume II: Sips of Wisdom From the Carpenter's Cup
Aventine Press 2006
The second edition of witty and powerful insights from the pen of Troy Brewer is sure to encourage and inspire readers. Be refreshed by reading this companion issue and a timeless testament to the power of God's voice through every day events.

Numbers That Preach: Understanding God's Mathematical Lingo
Aventine Press 2007
Your Bible, your history books, and even your newspaper headlines are full of God shouting a powerful message of hope and healing. The same author who designed 24,900 miles around the planet, also calculated 24 hours around your clock, and predetermined 24 elders around the throne. But unless you know what God is consistently speaking through the number 24, you miss the message. In fact, you don't even know there is a

message. Numbers That Preach is a fun look at the otherwise hidden sermons God is declaring through His mathematical lingo. For more than twenty years, author Troy Brewer has studied Biblical text and collected interesting facts, figures and statistics that show powerful meaning in the numbers around us.

Living Life /Forward: Discovering The Power of Supernatural Upgrade
Aventine Press 2013
LIVING LIFE /FORWARD is a collection of thoughts, Kingdom principles and fun supernatural revelation about our God given mandate to reach our fullest potential. God coded our DNA to be people attracted to the next level and generally happy with anything related to improvement. Troy Brewer skillfully takes you step by step and from faith to faith into unclaimed upgrade. Yes, your universe is still expanding and your Creator is cheering you on toward something much better. This book is going to help you accelerate your Journey toward the adventure of /Forward.

All of Troy's books can be found at Aventine press or online through Amazon and other fine book retailers.

ABOUT THE AUTHOR

Troy Brewer is something of minor league Renaissance man. A man of the cloth without the cloth, he is the founding Senior Pastor of OpenDoor Church in Burleson TX.

His nationally broadcasted Radio show, "Experiencing Real Life" is heard daily from coast to coast in the USA.

He is the Founder of the OpenDoor Food Bank, which gives away millions of pounds of food to tens of thousands of hurting people every year in North Central Texas.

As a professional musician his guitar has taken him to several continents and as a missionary his calling has taken him to at least 32 countries, many of them multiple times.

He has had audience, with the King of Uganda, Sir Richard Branson in the British Virgin Islands, The Governor of the State of Texas, multiple celebrities and even a brief encounter with The Queen of England in London.

He acts as a chaplain to professional musicians of all genres.

He supports his wife's effort to help hurting children all over the world through her organization which he is a board member.

SPARKWORLDWIDE.ORG

CPSIA information can be obtained
at www.ICGtesting.com
Printed in the USA
FSHW04n2115150318
45501FS